How to Go to Heaven for Teen Girls

Your Proven, Step-By-Step Plan to Achieve Eternal Salvation

A Save Your Soul Book

Mike Mains

Published by Friends of Fatima

Copyright © 2023 by Mike Mains. All Rights Reserved.

No part of this book may be used or reproduced in any manner, whatsoever, without written permission from the author. The exception being in cases of brief quotations embodied in critical articles or reviews. This book is intended for educational purposes only. The author and publisher bear no responsibility or liability whatsoever to any person or entity with respect to any loss, damage, or injury caused or alleged to be caused directly or indirectly by the information contained in this book.

The author is indebted to the Brothers of Most Holy Family Monastery whose work was instrumental in educating him on many of the issues discussed in this book.

All Bible quotes in this book except for one come from the King James Bible. The King James Bible is not the most accurate translation of the Bible, but it is the most popular. It was chosen to make it easier for readers to verify the information presented here.

Author contact: mainsmike@yahoo.com

Contents

Heaven is at Your Fingertips . . . 5
Is Heaven in Your Future? . . . 7
The Scientific Way to Heaven . . . 18
Do This and God Will Love You . . . 21
The Power of Prayer . . . 37
An Easy Way to Lead a Virtuous Life . . . 46
More Easy Ways to Lead a Virtuous Life . . . 63
God Wants You Here . . . 84
God *Doesn't* Want You Here . . . 97
The Truth Shall Set You Free . . . 138
Be the Woman God Wants You to Be . . . 150
Heaven—You're Almost There! . . . 179

Preface

Heaven is at Your Fingertips

Congratulations! You hold in your hands a book that's guaranteed to take you straight to Heaven!

Inside these power-packed pages are the exact steps you need to take if you wish to spend eternity in paradise. If you truly desire to go to Heaven, you're on your way.

If you're lukewarm about the afterlife, then I encourage you to read this book with the intention of strengthening your resolve.

If you don't believe in Heaven, you might want to ask yourself what brought you here. You didn't discover this book by accident. God brought you here for a reason. He wants you to see what's in these pages. He wants to make you aware of His infinite mercy and where you stand on the road to Heaven. Don't be frightened by that. It's actually a good thing.

Books are powerful. Reading this particular book could trigger a thought in your mind that ultimately leads to your eternal salvation. In other words, this book might make the difference between you going to Heaven or . . . to that other place. Nothing else you read or do for the rest of your life will ever be more important.

Some of what you read here will be quite startling. Therefore, I urge you to read with an open mind. Every statement in this book is sourced and documented for you to verify for yourself.

As you read you may find yourself drawing closer to God. That's good. It's a sign that you actually *are* drawing closer to God; a sign that this book was put into your hands expressly for that purpose.

> "Remember that it is not the multitude who are being saved, but the elect of God. Be not then affrighted at the great multitude of the people who are carried here and there by the winds like the waters of the sea."—Saint Basil, Letter 257

Chapter One

Is Heaven in Your Future?

Heaven.

The very word puts you at peace, doesn't it? Thoughts of Heaven relax the body and create images in the mind of wonder and joy. Indeed, just saying the word Heaven makes a person feel happy. Try it right now. Say, "Heaven." Don't you feel better already?

While Heaven is a world of eternal happiness, getting there is a different story. All available evidence (yes, we have evidence) suggests that no one goes to Heaven easily or without suffering, and that very few people make it there at all. That's a sobering thought. Heaven, our true home, is waiting for us, yet getting there is exceedingly difficult and *almost nobody* makes it.

So where does that leave us? Where does that leave you, me, and everyone else who longs to go to Heaven? It leaves us on the brink of a long and difficult journey. Not an impossible journey, but certainly a journey fraught with peril and one in which very few people succeed in reaching their desired destination. For those who do succeed, the reward is indescribable—eternity spent in Heaven.

In this book, you will find the most efficient plan possible for anyone who truly desires to go to Heaven to actually get there. I wrote this book especially for you. I want to see you in Heaven. I want to see everyone in Heaven. Sadly, that's not possible, but I hope to help as many people get to Heaven as I can. Will you be one of those people?

Four Simple Steps

The plan outlined in this book consists of four simple steps. For some people, these steps will be easy to follow. For others, they won't.

I'm sorry, but that's just the way it is. If going to Heaven was easy, everyone would be doing it.

Remember, too, as you read that we are dealing with facts, not fiction. Everything in this book is proven, verified, and documented. Everything here is backed by facts and evidence and laid out in clear and concise fashion for you to follow. In other words, we are dealing with truth. Not with what some people *think* is the truth. Not with what some people *wish* was the truth, but with actual truth.

You may have heard the expression "the truth hurts." There's a lot of truth in that statement. The truth *does* hurt. Society has become so fake and so full of lies that the truth actually hurts people. I mean that literally. When truth reveals something that people don't like, they experience actual physical pain to the point where they either run away from it or demand that it be shut down and censored.

Take the fundamental teachings of Christianity, which tell us that very few people go to Heaven and that in order to get there, certain Commandments must be followed. That little bit of truth right there freaks people out. When they hear it, they shriek like little girls and cover their ears. The truth actually hurts them. Some people reading this are experiencing pain right now.

Because so many people are hurt by the truth, we're no longer supposed to speak truthfully. We're supposed to lie in order not to "offend" people. We're supposed to pepper our speech with liberal platitudes, carefully designed to protect other people's feelings. We're supposed to do those things even if it means misleading others and providing them with false information that will send them straight to hell.

This book is different. It lays out the evidence regarding Heaven and lets you decide. Because that's the sticky thing about truth that few people want to face—when you pursue truth, you have to go all-in. You can't say, "I'll take this truth here, but not that truth there." You have to take *all* the truth and let the chips fall where they may. Even if the results are not to your liking. Almost nobody is willing to do that.

Almost nobody is willing to hear or accept truth that runs counter to what they've been programmed to believe. Most people, when confronted with such truths, will simply ignore them. They can't dispute the truths that offend them, so they pretend the truths don't exist. They do that no matter how conclusive the evidence is.

If you desire to go to Heaven, you will have to do the exact opposite of what everyone else in the world is doing. You will have to embrace truth and make choices based upon facts and evidence, rather than on opinion and emotion.

Facts and evidence have a habit of turning up uncomfortable truths—truths that make a person squirm, shudder, and shake; truths that are often frightening to face and impossible to ignore. One of those uncomfortable truths is the knowledge that very few people make it to Heaven. If you want to be among them and go to Heaven yourself, then you must believe and behave exactly as they do.

Or as Saint Anselm said: "If thou wouldst be certain of being in the number of the elect, strive to be one of the few, not of the many. And if thou wouldst be quite sure of thy salvation, strive to be among the fewest of the few."

Or as Saint Louis Marie de Montfort said: "Be one of the small number who find the way to life, and enter by the narrow gate into Heaven. Take care not to follow the majority and the common herd, so many of whom are lost."

Or as Saint John Climacus said: "Live with the few if you want to reign with the few."

Or as Saint Augustine said: "If you wish to imitate the multitude, then you shall not be among the few who shall enter by the narrow gate."

Few Are Saved

Once again, there are some people reading this—not you, of course—who are foaming at the mouth right now and ready to throw this book across the room. Hearing that very few people are saved sends them into spastic rage. They're not angry out of compassion for humanity. It's not that at all. They're angry because they know that they themselves are on the road to hell. Yet what good does it do to rail against reality?

Anger at knowing that very few people are saved stems from pride, and pride has a way of blinding people to the truth, most often with devastating results. It prevents those who are following a false path from admitting that they're wrong. It literally deprives them of Heaven.

Personally, I've never had a problem with admitting I was wrong. Growing up, I believed every lie they taught me in school.

I believed the Civil War was fought over slavery.

I believed Germany started World War II.

I believed in the germ theory of disease.

I believed that Jesus and all of the Apostles were Jews.

You name it, I believed it. When I discovered later that all of those beliefs (and many more) were lies, I immediately admitted I was wrong. Naturally, I was dismayed to a point, but I wasn't ashamed at being duped, because I didn't blame myself. I blamed the people who lied to me. If you've been misled, as I was, I encourage you to take the same attitude.

The sad truth, for those with the courage to accept it, is that very few souls are saved. *Very* few. How do we know that? First, we have the Bible:

Luke 13:23-24: "Then said one unto him, Lord, are there few that be saved? And he said unto them, Strive to enter in at the straight gate: for many, I say unto you, will seek to enter in, and shall not be able."

Luke 13:28: "There shall be weeping and gnashing of teeth, when ye shall see Abraham, and Isaac, and Jacob, and all the prophets, in the kingdom of God, and you yourselves thrust out."

Matthew 7:13-14: "Enter ye in at the straight gate: for wide is the gate, and broad is the way, that leadeth to destruction, and many there be which go in thereat: Because straight is the gate, and narrow is the way, which leadeth unto life: and few there be that find it."

Matthew 22:13-14: "Bind him hand and foot, and take him away, and cast him into outer darkness; there shall be weeping and gnashing of teeth. For many are called, but few are chosen."

We also have the Doctors of the Church:

Saint Augustine: "Few are saved in comparison to those who are damned."

Saint John Chrysostom: "How many of the inhabitants of this city may perhaps be saved? What I am about to tell you is very terrible, yet I will not conceal it from you. Out of this thickly populated city with its thousands of inhabitants not one hundred people will be saved. I even doubt whether there will be as many as that!"

We have history, which tells us that in the time of Noah the entire world was submerged and only eight people were deemed worthy enough to survive.

History also tells us that only four people escaped the fire of Sodom and one of them was turned into a pillar of salt.

We have Divine Revelation, such as the apparitions of Fatima in 1917, where the young seers were shown a vision of hell and told that hell is where the majority of people go. (Fatima is also where the Miracle of the Sun took place on October 13, 1917, one of the greatest miracles in the history of the world.)

We have the word of Jacinta Marto, one of the three seers of Fatima, to whom it was revealed, twenty years before the fact, that almost everyone slated to die in World War II would be going to hell, regardless of how they died or which side they were on: "Of the war that is going to come. So many people are going to die. And almost all of them are going to hell." (*Our Lady of Fatima* by William Thomas Walsh)

Between the Bible, the teachings of the Church fathers, history, and Divine Revelation, we have plenty of facts and evidence that all tell us that very few people make it to Heaven. At the same time, we have zero evidence to the contrary; zero evidence that most people are saved.

The Few, the Just, and the Damned

Why are so many people condemned to spend eternity in hell, while only a handful of souls are saved? We'll explore that question throughout this book. But bear in mind that to ask why so few souls are saved is pointless. It's like asking why the sky is blue or why the grass is green. Reality is what it is. Asking why doesn't change anything.

If you doubt that so many mortal creatures could fall from grace and condemn themselves to hell, consider that roughly one third of the angels in Heaven rebelled against God and were cast out. If such a large number of angels—angels far holier than humans—could fall from grace and be cast out of Heaven, then how hard is it to imagine that 95% or more of the world's population might do the same?

Consider also that the angels were already in Heaven. They didn't face the same temptations that humans do on earth in this sinful world we live in. Yet those angels still fell from grace. And they fell for the same reason that the majority of people fall—envy and pride.

Your ultimate goal in life is not to "follow your dreams." It's not to find your "soul mate," or to pursue happiness here on earth. Your mission, should you decide to accept it, is to make sure that you are one of the few who are saved.

With that in mind, you must do everything you can—everything in your power—to ensure your salvation. Whether or not you succeed depends on the strength of your desire.

To want to go to Heaven is not enough.

Everyone *wants* to go to Heaven. However, to want something is often little more than a wish. A person who merely wants something is almost never willing to make the necessary sacrifices and lifestyle changes needed to get what they say they want.

Desire is different. A person who truly desires something *will* make the necessary sacrifices and lifestyle changes. They'll make those changes in the blink of an eye, because the thing they desire means everything to them.

If you have a strong desire to go to Heaven—and you wouldn't be reading this book if you didn't—then you're already halfway there. All that's left is for you to arrange your life in the way that God wants.

Age is Irrelevant

Don't put off the importance of Heaven because of your age. It's hard to think about death when you're young, but today young people are dying in droves, thanks to the fake vaccine for the phony virus. If you took it, you could be one of them. (If you took any type of vaccine or even the nasal swab test you could be one of them.) Don't delay another second. Get your afterlife in order immediately. Start that process by reading this book and doing what it suggests.

Habits formed in childhood follow us into our teens, and habits formed in our teens follow us into adulthood. The type of life you're leading now is the type of life you'll likely lead as an adult. Now, there are exceptions. I'm a much different person today than I was as a teen. I've changed considerably.

But I'm the exception that proves the rule. Virtually everyone I grew up with is the exact same now as they were then. Not one of them has changed in any way. Who they were when I knew them as children, as teens, or as young adults, is who they are now.

Even worse, many of them are now dead and I have no doubt they are now in hell. I wish that weren't the case, but all available evidence suggests that it is. Of the people I grew up with who are still living, almost all of them appear headed for hell when they die. Again, I wish that weren't the case, but I see no way out of it for them. Unless they make drastic changes in their life, and none of them are willing to do that, they're all going to hell.

So here's an early lesson you can take from this book—people don't change. If they're slaves to the world now, they'll be slaves to the world on the day they die. For you personally that means if you want to go to Heaven, start on the path today. Don't put it off a second longer.

Words of Hope, Meant Just for You

This book is not for the squeamish. Reading it will be a frightening experience. That's good in a sense because fear is a tremendous motivator. But no matter how frightened you become while reading this book, take comfort in the fact that I am with you every step of the way. Far more importantly, God is with you. He wants you to succeed. Never forget that.

Are you ready to begin the incredible journey from earth to Heaven?

If so, then let me extend my hand across the time and space that separates us and take your hand in mine.

Together, we sally forth.

Together, we save our souls from eternal damnation.

Together, we go to Heaven.

"The following narrative from Saint Vincent Ferrer will show you what you may think about it. He relates that an archdeacon in Lyons gave up his charge and retreated to a desert place to do penance, and that he died the same day and hour as Saint Bernard. After his death, he appeared to his bishop and said to him, 'Know Monsignor that at the very hour I passed away, thirty-three thousand people also died. Out of this number, Bernard and myself went up to Heaven without delay, three went to purgatory, and all the others fell into hell.' "—Saint Leonard of Port Maurice, *The Little Number of Those Who Are Saved*

Chapter Two

The Scientific Way to Heaven

Is there a science to going to Heaven? You bet there is, and it's as certain a science as math or geometry. The science of math says if you add two plus two, you get four. That's indisputable. Using the science of math you cannot fail.

The science of Heaven is no different. It says if you follow a handful of specific steps, you will go to Heaven. That, too, is indisputable. Using the science of Heaven you cannot fail.

In this book you will learn just what the science of Heaven is and how you can use it to guarantee yourself an eternity in paradise. Just as the science of math is foolproof, so is the science of Heaven. Apply it correctly and you cannot fail. Let's start with some basics.

Whatever your goal in life is, the best way to get there is to find someone who has already achieved what to achieve and mirror them. In other words, find a mentor and repeat what they have done.

The easiest way to learn how to do that is to ask them for help. However, even if they are unable or unwilling to share their knowledge with you, it's still possible to learn from them by studying their life and reading their books. They've done the heavy lifting. They've shown you the way. All you have to do is follow in their footsteps.

Now if the thing you want to accomplish has never been done before, you'll have to be the first and blaze the trail. But in this book we're concerned with going to Heaven, which is something that other people *have* done before.

Beginning with the Apostles in first century A.D., up to and including Padre Pio, the holiest man of the 20th century, we have hundreds of examples of people that we know with a high degree of certainty are now in Heaven. People that have already achieved what we want to achieve.

Not only that, but there are commonalities among them, certain things they all did in order to go to Heaven and certain things they all didn't do. If we wish to go to Heaven ourselves, all we have to do is incorporate those same practices into our own lives. By following in their footsteps and living our lives exactly as they lived theirs, we are guaranteed to get the same results. We are guaranteed to go to Heaven. What more could a Heaven-seeker ask for?

These Heavenly mentors didn't just leave us a trail of bread crumbs to follow either, they left us an entire system; a system that couldn't be more complete. Every doubt, every question that one might have, they've already addressed and answered in full.

Sounds simple, right? It is, and yet it isn't.

It's simple in the sense that yes, others have shown us the way. They've provided us with a road map—a treasure map, if you will—and all we have to do is follow it.

It isn't simple because it requires us to make changes in our lives in order to go to Heaven. Our mentors in Heaven have shown us what to do if we wish to follow them, but we still have to do what they've shown us.

So where do we start? What is it that those who are already in Heaven have done that we must also do if we wish to join them? There are four commonalities among them; four things that they all did and that the great majority of people don't do. In order to go to Heaven, we must do those same four things.

To find out what they are; to learn what the first thing is that a person must do if they wish to go to Heaven, simply turn to the next page.

Words of Hope, Meant Just for You

I congratulate you for reading this far. It shows that you really are serious about going to Heaven. You can do it. I know you can do it. Master the four steps you're about to read in the coming pages and Heaven is yours.

> "What a precious science to know how to walk in the way of salvation, and to adopt the means of attaining eternal life."—Saint Alphonsus Liguori, *Preparation for Death*

Chapter Three

Do This and God Will Love You

Stop sinning. That's the first step one must take in order to go to Heaven.

From the early Apostles to the saints who followed them, every person that we know with a high degree of certainty is now in Heaven—all of them, without exception—did everything they could to lead a sinless life, and they all preached the need to stop sinning.

You can do the same.

In fact, if you want to go to Heaven, you *must* do the same. You won't get there if you don't.

Every time we sin, we dig ourselves deeper into a hole—a hole that brings us closer to hell and further away from Heaven. The moment we stop sinning is the moment we start to reverse course.

Now what if you've dug yourself into a hole of sin so deep that it looks like you'll never climb out? The answer is simple: put the shovel down and stop digging. In other words, stop sinning. As long as you're alive, you have the ability to turn things around and climb out of the hole you've dug for yourself. Refraining from sin is the first step one must take in order to go to Heaven.

Heaven and Sin are Not Compatible

The need to stop sinning in order to go to Heaven is one of those uncomfortable truths that people don't want to hear; one of those truths that cause people to experience actual physical pain.

That's because most people, for whatever reason, don't want to give up their sins. And because they don't want to give up their sins, they will engage in all manner of mental gymnastics in order to avoid doing so.

People who do this fall primarily into two camps. The first is the "but I'm a nice person" camp, and the second is the "saved by faith alone" camp.

"But I'm a Nice Person"

There are plenty of people who believe that because they are "nice" they will automatically go to Heaven when they die. They say things like, "But I'm a nice person. As long as I don't kill anyone, I should go to Heaven," as if their wishing it were true actually made it so. People who fall into this camp have only a vague notion of the afterlife, because they never think about it. They're too preoccupied pursuing money, fame, romance, and sex to think about anything else.

In the rare moments when the thought of an afterlife does cross their mind, they concede they that are guilty of numerous sins. However, they figure that as long as they don't kill anyone or commit theft on a massive scale, God will allow them into Heaven. They couldn't be more wrong.

The belief that someone will go to Heaven because they're a nice person is actually quite common. Everyone in my immediate family believes this, as do most of the people I know. The problem with holding such a belief is that it's simply not true.

One of the reasons why so many people fall into the "but I'm a nice person" camp is because we live in a permissive society. The average person believes that if something is legal and considered normal by society's standards, then by natural extension it must also be morally acceptable and pleasing to God.

Take the sin of homosexuality. The average person sees that homosexuality is not only legal, but normalized and heavily promoted by society. As a result, they believe that it must also be morally acceptable and not a sin to engage in.

The average person does this with a whole host of sins, including abortion, drug use, reading and watching pornography, sex outside of marriage, masturbation, birth control, immodest dress, usury, reading romance novels, buying and selling on Sundays, and more.

If you tell them that just because something is legal, that doesn't mean it's not a sin, you'll be met with a fluoride stare. The idea that something could be both legal and heavily promoted on television, yet remain a sin, and not just any sin, but a sin that will send a person straight to hell, is simply incomprehensible to the average person. It's too much for their limited minds to grasp.

Those who push for more and more permissiveness know this and it's why they keep pushing. Their actions are less an attempt to undermine society as they are a coordinated attack on Christianity, with the intent to send as many souls to hell as possible.

We're at the point now in American society where large swaths of people believe it's perfectly acceptable to riot, loot, and shoplift. After all, they've had decades of media and academic indoctrination telling them that society owes them the very things they are stealing.

They can also see with their own eyes that if these acts were wrong in any way, then society would punish them for it. Instead, society condones such activity and actually promotes it. None of this is by accident. All of it is intentional.

You Can Be Nice and Still Go to Hell

There were nice people around at the time of Noah, but they were also sinners. God didn't spare any of them.

Not everyone living in Sodom was a homosexual. But those who weren't, allowed the sin of homosexuality to flourish. Just like today, they shrugged their shoulders and said, "Whatever floats your boat," or "Love is love." Just like today, they thought they were being nice. God destroyed them all.

When I was in the movie business almost everyone I met fell into the "but I'm a nice person" camp. They smiled and invited you into their homes. They showed intense interest in every facet of your life. And yet they were all incorrigible sinners. Homosexuality was rampant. So was immodest dress, abortion, and drug use. Everyone slept with everyone. Everyone got high with everyone. But they were nice people.

God wants us to be nice, obviously, but more importantly, God wants us to obey His Commandments. If we sin and fail to obey God's Commandments, then it doesn't matter at all how nice we are.

Nowhere in the Bible does God say, "Yes, my child, continue to get drunk and watch pornography, continue to dress immodestly and read your trashy romance novels, continue to lust after celebrities and sin as much as you please, as long as you're nice to others you can still go to Heaven." On the contrary, what the Bible says is:

> 1 Corinthians 6:9-10: "Know ye not that the unrighteous shall not inherit the kingdom of God? Be not deceived: neither fornicators, nor idolaters, nor adulterers, nor effeminate, nor abusers of themselves with mankind, nor thieves, nor covetous, nor drunkards, nor revilers, nor extortioners, shall inherit the kingdom of God."

> Galatians 5:19-21: "Now the works of the flesh are manifest, which are these; Adultery, fornication, uncleanness, lasciviousness, idolatry, witchcraft,

hatred, variance, emulations, wrath, strife, seditions, heresies, envyings, murders, drunkenness, revellings, and such like: of the which I tell you before, as I have also told you in time past, that they which do such things shall not inherit the kingdom of God."

Are you surprised by all of the sins that are included on those lists? I was the first time I read them. Saint Paul says a person can go to hell for drunkenness, fornication, witchcraft, and a whole lot more. Perhaps you don't practice witchcraft, but do you play with Tarot cards? Do you read horoscopes or Harry Potter books? Do you own an Ouija board? Those are all different forms of witchcraft.

And did you know that masturbation is a mortal sin that will send a person straight to hell? On page 52 of the book *The Bible Proves the Teaching of the Catholic Church,* Brother Peter Dimond writes: "According to St. Thomas Aquinas, the sin of 'uncleanness' or 'effeminacy' (which excludes one from Heaven) is the mortal sin of masturbation."

Note also the phrase "abusers of themselves with mankind" that Saint Paul uses. If you look up the word "abusers," as it is used here in *Strong's Concordance*, a book that lists the original Greek and Hebrew translations for every word in the King James Bible, it means sodomite.

Saint Peter Damian in Chapter Two of his landmark work *The Book of Gomorrah* interprets the word "sodomite" as including the sin of masturbation, which he condemns in the harshest language possible.

If you didn't know before that masturbation was a mortal sin, you do now. A person who masturbates today and dies tomorrow, without receiving the Sacrament of Confession, is going straight to hell.

Yet masturbation is now being taught in schools all across the country to children as young as four and five. That's not an accident and it's not being done strictly because the teachers are sickos and perverts, which they are. It's being done to intentionally groom children into engaging in masturbation and homosexuality in order to damn their souls to hell.

By the way, if you find yourself in a conversation or written exchange with someone who falsely claims that masturbation is not a mortal sin; be aware that the person you're communicating with is most likely a slave to lust and addicted to this most vile of sins.

If you yourself are addicted to masturbation, keep reading, because the following three chapters after this one contain some astoundingly successful advice on how to stop sinning. Before we get to that, however, I want to say a few words about the belief that one is "saved" by faith alone.

All You Need is Faith?

Those who believe in faith alone say that sin is irrelevant. They say that as long as you believe in Jesus Christ, then you are "saved." And if you are "saved," you can sin all you want and still go to Heaven. That doctrine runs counter to common sense. It says you can molest, murder, and rape your way through life and still go to Heaven, as long as you believe in Jesus. Sort of like a "Get Out of Hell Free" card.

The belief in faith alone actually makes less sense than those who say, "But I'm a nice person." The latter camp at least acknowledges that there are serious sins—like murder—they just believe that as long as they avoid those major sins and treat everyone nice they will go to Heaven.

The faith alone crowd goes even further than that. They say that all sin is immediately forgiven, that as long as you believe in Jesus Christ you are "saved." Then they cover themselves by adding that a person who commits serious sin—such as adultery, massive theft, or murder—was never a believer in the first place.

But that's simply not true. I've believed in Jesus Christ my entire life, yet there were plenty of times, particularly in my teens and twenties, when I committed mortal sin, yet I never stopped believing in Jesus. I never stopped praying.

I belonged to the "but I'm a nice person" camp. Because I was honest, smiled at children, and fed stray cats, I thought I was immune from hell. Surely, a little fornication wouldn't keep me out of Heaven. After all, look at how nice I treated everyone. Thank God I didn't die at the time. If I had, I'd be roasting in hell right now and for all eternity.

Look at the Apostles on the night and early morning of Jesus' passion. Peter not only lied, he denied Jesus three times—both very serious sins—does that mean he was never a believer to begin with?

The other Apostles ran away when Jesus was arrested. The only Apostle who showed up at the Crucifixion was

John. Does that mean none of those other Apostles were believers to begin with?

Take a look at what Saint Paul writes in 1 Timothy 4:1: "Now the Spirit speaketh expressly, that in the latter times some shall depart from the faith, giving heed to seducing spirits, and doctrines of devils."

Right there Saint Paul says that people can have faith, yet depart from it by committing sin. He doesn't say they never had faith to begin with.

In 1 Timothy 6:10, Saint Paul writes, "For the love of money is the root of all evil: which while some coveted after, they have erred from the faith, and pierced themselves through with many sorrows."

Saint Paul makes the same point, saying that one can err from the faith by committing sin. He never says such a person never had faith to begin with. What else does the King James Bible say about faith alone?

> James 2:20: "But wilt thou know, O vain man, that faith without works is dead?"

It doesn't get much clearer than that. This lone quote from Saint James pretty much obliterates the concept of faith alone.

Notice also that the saint calls those who believe in faith alone "vain." Vanity is a sign of bad will, which we'll discuss a little later.

James 2:14: "What doth it profit, my brethren, though a man say he hath faith, and have not works? Can faith save him?"

That quote is another knockout punch.

Matthew: 19:16-21: "And, behold, one came and said unto him, Good Master, what good thing shall I do, that I may have eternal life?

"And he said unto him, Why callest thou me good? There is none good but one, that is, God: but if thou wilt enter into life, keep the commandments.

"He saith unto him, Which? Jesus said, Thou shalt do no murder, Thou shalt not commit adultery, Thou shalt not steal, Thou shalt not bear false witness,

"Honor thy father and thy mother: and, Thou shalt love thy neighbor as thyself."

In this passage, Jesus blows the belief in faith alone out of the water. He specifically tells one of his followers to keep the Ten Commandments in order to go to Heaven. In fact, Jesus mentions the Ten Commandments again in John 14:15: "If ye love me, keep my commandments."

Yet believers in the doctrine of faith alone say the Ten Commandments are irrelevant; that a person can sin all he wants and still go to Heaven.

Remember the woman taken in adultery?

> John 8:10-11: "Woman, where are those thine accusers? Hath no man condemned thee? She said, No man, Lord. And Jesus said unto her, Neither do I condemn thee: go and sin no more."

If faith alone is all we need to go to Heaven, why did Jesus tell her, "Go and sin no more"? He didn't say, "Go and have faith alone," he told her specifically not to sin.

If faith alone is all we need to go to Heaven, why did Jesus specifically tell us in the Lord's Prayer, "Forgive us our trespasses, as we forgive those who trespass against us, and lead us not into temptation, but deliver us from evil"?

Why do we need to be forgiven if sins don't matter?

Why do we need to pray to be delivered from evil if sins don't count?

If we can obtain salvation through faith alone, why did Jesus institute the Sacrament of Confession and bestow upon the Apostles the power to forgive sins?

> John 20:23: "Whose soever sins ye remit, they are remitted unto them; and whose soever sins ye retain, they are retained."

The Sacrament of Confession becomes meaningless if faith alone is all that's required. After all, if sin is irrelevant, then why does anyone need to confess and receive absolution?

Yet Jesus specifically gave the power to forgive sins to the Apostles and their successors.

If faith alone is all that's necessary in order to go to Heaven, why do we need to work out our salvation with fear and trembling?

> Philippians 2:12: "Wherefore, my beloved, as ye have always obeyed, not as in my presence only, but now much more in my absence, work out your own salvation with fear and trembling."

If faith alone were all that one needed, why did Jesus warn his Apostles not to give in to temptation?

> Luke 22:40: "And when he was at the place, he said unto them, Pray that ye enter not into temptation."

If faith alone was enough to get us into Heaven, why did Saint Paul tell us to avoid fornication?

> 1 Corinthians 6:18: "Flee fornication."

If faith alone is all we need, why does Saint Paul repeatedly list whole multitudes of sins, one after the other, and tell us that committing any one of those sins will keep us out of Heaven?

> 1 Corinthians 6:9-10: "Know ye not that the unrighteous shall not inherit the kingdom of God? Be not deceived: neither fornicators, nor idolaters, nor

adulterers, nor effeminate, nor abusers of themselves with mankind, nor thieves, nor covetous, nor drunkards, nor revilers, nor extortioners, shall inherit the kingdom of God."

Galatians 5:19-21: "Now the works of the flesh are manifest, which are these; Adultery, fornication, uncleanness, lasciviousness, idolatry, witchcraft, hatred, variance, emulations, wrath, strife, seditions, heresies, envyings, murders, drunkenness, revellings, and such like: of the which I tell you before, as I have also told you in time past, that they which do such things shall not inherit the kingdom of God."

Can you see how the Bible utterly destroys the false position of faith alone? It contains literally dozens of passages all telling us that sinners, regardless of what they believe, will not enter the Kingdom of Heaven.

The Bible is a book of behavior, instructing us to do these things here, but not those things there. Yet, the faith alone crowd would have us dismiss what the Bible says as rubbish.

There does not exist anywhere in history a single saint or mystic that we know with a high degree of certainty is now in Heaven who said we could get there through faith alone or by being a nice person. On the contrary, they are unanimous on insisting that in order to go to Heaven, a person must refrain from sin. To assume that one can sin and still go to Heaven is a false interpretation of God's infinite mercy. Yes, God is merciful, but as Saint Alphonsus writes, "Great as his mercy, how many does he every day send to hell?" (*The Sermons of St. Alphonsus Liguori*, Sermon XIV)

The Blessed Virgin Mary says, "And his mercy is on them that fear him from generation to generation." (Luke 1:50)

Those who put their trust in God's mercy, but continue to sin are showing God by their actions that they do not fear Him. And if that's the case, why should God extend to them any mercy at all? People who continue to sin are making a mockery of God's mercy.

Do you really think that someone who reads or watches pornography, who masturbates, who dresses immodestly, who gossips and lies, who engages in sex outside of marriage, who commits any of a number of sins is going to just waltz right into Heaven?

I wouldn't bet on it. Yet those who stake their afterlife on the false belief of faith alone are doing just that. They're taking an enormous gamble. Look at it this way: If you base your life on the belief that you will go to Heaven regardless of your sins, either because you're a nice person or because you believe in the concept of faith alone, and it turns out you're wrong, you're doomed. You'll burn in hell for all eternity.

On the other hand, if you accept what the Bible teaches and base your life around the belief that in order to go to Heaven a person must refrain from committing sin, and thus you die in a state of grace, and it turns out you're wrong, you haven't lost anything. You're still in Heaven.

Belief in the former—faith alone or "but I'm a nice person"—is a gamble that can send a person straight to hell, while belief in the latter—refraining from sin—is a sure thing that will send a person straight to Heaven. Which approach is smarter?

Rather than taking the unbiblical position of faith alone or "but I'm a nice person," it might be better to ask yourself, "Does my way of living please God?" For those committing any type of sin, the answer is no.

Words of Hope, Meant Just for You

If you've read this far, give yourself a pat on the back. Most people, upon learning that they must give up their sins in order to go to Heaven, stopped reading long ago. But you didn't. That makes you a prime candidate for Heaven.

For anyone who has read this far, yet fails to see the necessity of refraining from sin in order to go to Heaven, I recommend treating yourself to a crash course in Christian education. You can do that by visiting the website www.MostHolyFamilyMonastery.com

They are the world's foremost experts on Christian theology. Read their articles, binge-watch their videos, and immerse yourself in true Christian doctrine. Once you start you won't be able to stop. That's how compelling their information is.

Now that we've established the need to stop sinning in order to go to Heaven, let's look at the best ways to do that. The next three chapters contain excellent advice on how to avoid sin and lead a virtuous life.

No matter how deep of a hole you've dug yourself into, you can climb your way out and join the saints in Heaven.

That you're reading this book is a sign that God wants you to do just that. Remember, too, that I'm with you on this journey. I want to see you in Heaven.

"Of that ignorance which makes the sinner say, What harm have I done? What great evil is that sin which I have committed? God is merciful—he pardons sinners. What an insult! What temerity! What blindness!"—Saint Alphonsus Liguori, *Preparation for Death*

Chapter Four

The Power of Prayer

Avoiding sin is the first commonality among everyone that we know with a high degree of certainty is now in Heaven. The second commonality among them is daily and consistent prayer.

They all prayed daily, and they all recommended daily and consistent prayer as the best way in the world to resist temptation and avoid sin.

In fact, when it comes to conquering sin, prayer is your secret weapon. No matter how strong you are, without daily and consistent prayer you're apt to fall into sin again and again.

You can try leading a holy life without prayer, but your odds of succeeding are slim. Truth be told, I'm not sure if it's even possible for someone to lead a life of holiness while avoiding prayer.

How much prayer, you ask? My first inclination is to say that any amount of prayer, even five minutes, is better than none. However, my second inclination, and it's based upon studying the lives of those whom we know with a high degree of certainty are now in Heaven, is that we should all be praying a minimum of one hour a day.

Some of you reading that will react with a huff and say it's simply not possible to devote that much time every day to prayer. To which I would reply that it depends on how serious you are about going to Heaven. If your desire to go to Heaven is strong, you'll find the time to pray for an hour every day, and remember, that's the minimum.

Everyone that we know with a high degree of certainty is now in Heaven prayed for at least an hour every day. If you can't do the same, if you can't give at least one hour a day to prayer, then your odds of going to Heaven shrink considerably. They shrink for the simple reason that without that hour of prayer it's going to be very hard for you to resist temptation and avoid sin.

If you can't give at least *thirty minutes a day* to prayer—the approximate time it takes to say five decades of the Rosary—then you may as well throw in the towel. I hate to say that, but it's true.

To say, "I'm too busy," or "I don't have time for that," is an affront to God. You can make the time if you want to.

Saint Alphonsus speaks to this when he says, "All the elect are saved by prayer; all the damned are lost by neglect of prayer."

If even thirty minutes a day of prayer is too much for you then approach it in the same way that you would if you were starting a new exercise program. By that I mean begin with what you can comfortably do and work your way up. If you decided to start running, you wouldn't start out by running five miles on your first day. You'd start with what you could comfortably manage, probably a quarter mile or less, and work your way up from there. It's the same with prayer.

If five minutes a day of prayer is all you can muster in the beginning, so be it. Start with that and stick to it. Then when you're ready increase it to ten minutes a day. Then fifteen minutes a day, and so on. Before long you'll be up to thirty minutes a day. And when you're able to pray for thirty minutes a day, the jump to an hour a day is as easy as pie.

If you're struggling with the temptation and allurement of sin, then an hour a day (or more) of prayer is essential. Without it, you'll lack the spiritual strength to resist temptation, and find yourself prone to repeating the same sins over and over. You'll be like a hamster on a treadmill, spinning endlessly, but going nowhere.

Daily and consistent prayer will strengthen your resolve and make it easier for you to resist temptation and avoid sin. And the one method of prayer that has helped more people conquer sin than any other is the Rosary.

Just how powerful is the Rosary?

Saint Louis De Montfort says it will save your very soul—no matter what your present state of life is.

> "If you say the Rosary faithfully until death, I do assure you that, in spite of the gravity of your sins, you shall receive a never fading crown of glory. Even if you are on the brink of damnation, even if you have one

foot in hell, even if you have sold your soul to the devil as sorcerers do who practice black magic, and even if you are a heretic as obstinate as a devil, sooner or later you will be converted and amend your life and save your soul, if—and mark well what I say—if you say the Holy Rosary devoutly every day until death for the purpose of knowing the truth and obtaining contrition and pardon for your sins."—Saint Louis De Montfort, *The Secret of the Rosary*

There is no sin that can stand up to the power of the Rosary. If you're addicted to sin of any kind and wish to break its hold over you, praying the Rosary will do that. Relief will come quickly, but you must do your part. You must pray the Rosary every day.

The Rosary is especially effective in combating sins of impurity. If that is your weakness, if you are under constant assault from thoughts of impurity and the temptation to commit mortal sin, then praying the Rosary is your key to salvation.

It takes twenty-five minutes to say five decades of the Rosary (longer if you do it with full concentration) and over an hour to say all fifteen decades. So if you pray all fifteen decades, there's your hour a day of prayer right there, which, by the way, doesn't have to be done all at once. It can be broken up into two or more segments.

It can also be done when you're out walking or driving in your car. It can be done while riding the bus. It can be done silently while standing in line. You can buy a cheap plastic

Rosary for a dollar or two and carry one in your pocket, making it possible for you to say the Rosary anywhere.

If you truly wish to go to Heaven, and you wouldn't be reading this book if you didn't, begin praying the Rosary at once and continue doing so until the day you die.

A Miracle of the Rosary (One of Many)

Countless miracles have been attributed to praying the Rosary, and one of the most incredible miracles occurred in 1945.

As World War II drew to a close, the Japanese high command made numerous attempts to surrender, but all of their offers were rebuffed by the Truman administration. Instead of accepting Japan's surrender, on March 9 and 10, 1945, the United States military firebombed Tokyo, Japan, a civilian target populated mainly by children. Over 100,000 people were burned alive. It was the single most destructive bombing raid in history.

Then in August of the same year, despite even more offers of surrender from Japan, the United States military atom-bombed the cities of Hiroshima and Nagasaki, Japan. (Some credible researchers say that neither city was atom-bombed, but rather hit with a combination of napalm and mustard gas.)

Both Hiroshima and Nagasaki were civilian targets with no military value and both cities were populated mainly by Christian children. Nagasaki was so heavily populated with Christians, it was known as the Japanese Vatican.

The Hiroshima bombing killed 80,000 people instantly and another 50,000 died later from wounds and radiation. President Harry Truman, a 33rd degree Grand Master Freemason, boasted of the bombing, "Man has learned to produce the power of the sun here on earth."

Among the only survivors of the Hiroshima bombing were four Jesuit priests, Hugo Lassalie, Hubert Schiffer, Wilhelm Klensorge, and Hubert Cieslik. They lived only eight blocks from ground zero where the bomb detonated. They were praying the Rosary at the exact time when the bomb hit and they credited the Rosary for their survival. Everyone else within a square mile was instantly killed.

Not only did the four priests survive, they suffered only minor scratches and lived for years afterwards. They were examined over 200 times and no trace of radiation was ever found on any of them. Their building was the only one for miles around that wasn't demolished by the blast.

If praying the Rosary can save the lives of four men from an atom bomb, while everyone else around them is instantly killed, imagine what it can do for you and what a powerful weapon it can be in your battle to conquer sin.

Here's something else about the Rosary that very few people know. When you pray the Rosary consistently and strive to lead a sinless life, you develop over time the ability to tell truth from lies; to immediately spot when someone is lying to you and when they are telling the truth.

I call it the grace of discernment. It's a tremendous blessing and one which I can personally vouch for. I don't even have to be in the same room with a person. All I have to do is hear their voice or see them in a video and I can instantly tell whether they are telling the truth or not.

You might experience the same results. If so, no one will ever be able to lie to you again.

Mystics like Padre Pio were so advanced in this grace that they had the ability to read souls and hearts. Padre Pio could read a person's heart and instantly tell what sins they had committed and whether they were headed for Heaven or hell.

Saint Vincent Ferrer was also adept at reading souls and hearts. John of Plascenia, who accompanied Saint Vincent on his travels, said the saint could read souls like an open book. Sadly, I know of no one today who is able to do this.

Both Saint Vincent and Padre Pio prayed the Rosary constantly.

Lucy Santos was one of the three seers of Fatima where the Miracle of the Sun took place on October 13, 1917. Lucy later became a nun and was known as Sister Lucy or Sister Lucia. During this time, she was visited by both Our Lady and Our Lord. Shortly before her disappearance around the year 1960, Sister Lucy gave an interview to Father Fuentes in which she said the following about the Rosary:

> "Look, Father, the Most Holy Virgin in these last times in which we live has given a new efficacy to the recitation of the Holy Rosary. She has given this efficacy to such an extent that there is no problem, no matter how difficult it is, whether temporal or above all, spiritual, in the personal life of each one of us, of

our families, of the families of the world, or of the religious communities, or even of the life of peoples and nations that cannot be solved by the Rosary. There is no problem I tell you, no matter how difficult it is, that we cannot resolve by the prayer of the Holy Rosary. With the Holy Rosary, we will save ourselves. We will sanctify ourselves. We will console Our Lord and obtain the salvation of many souls."

You can read more about Fatima and the Miracle of the Sun that took place there in the book *Our Lady of Fatima* by William Thomas Walsh, and you can read more about Sister Lucy and the truth of what happened to her in my book *The Impostor Sister Lucy*. I recommend reading both, particularly the Walsh book.

If you're serious about leading a sinless life, then praying the Rosary is a must. Don't neglect this most vital step on the road to Heaven.

Words of Hope, Meant Just for You

Prayer has the potential to turn your life around. With it, you can soften your journey here on earth and prepare your soul for Heaven.

Don't let the recommendation of an hour a day put you off. It's okay to start slow (five minutes a day) and build up.

Put daily and consistent prayer, which includes praying the Rosary, first on your list when it comes to combating sin. And never stop praying.

The second item on your list when it comes to conquering sin is to avoid the corrupting influence of other people. We will address that most urgent of issues in the very next chapter.

"It is, above all, necessary to persevere in prayer till death, and never to cease to pray."—Saint Alphonsus Liguori, *The Sermons of St. Alphonsus Liguori*

Chapter Five

An Easy Way to Lead a Virtuous Life

The number one cause of sin in the world is other people. Therefore, if you're serious about going to Heaven, you must purge sinful people from your life.

To better understand this, stop for a moment and ask yourself how many times have you committed sin when left on your own, and how many times have you sinned due to the influence of others?

Who gave you your first cigarette?

Your first beer?

Your first hit on a joint?

Who introduced you to pornography?

Who taught you to cuss and swear?

Who taught you to gossip?

Who encouraged you to shoplift and steal?

Who seduced you?

Who said or did something that caused you to have an impure thought?

Who wronged you and made you seek vengeance?

Whose likeness have you committed sin to?

Who influenced you to dress immodestly? (Someone gave you the idea, either someone you know or someone you saw and you decided to imitate them.)

As you can see, in almost every case we've sinned due to the influence of someone else. If left alone, we probably would not have sinned.

Thus, it makes sense that after committing yourself to daily and consistent prayer, your first order of business is to avoid anyone that currently has or could have a corrupting influence on your life.

Saint Alphonsus likens this process to a ship caught in a stormy sea. Your ship's destination is the port of Heaven, but all around you, other ships are being tossed by the wind and waves. Many are sinking.

"When the tempest is violent," writes the saint, "and each person on board throws his goods into the sea in order to save his life. O folly of sinners, who, in the midst of such great dangers of eternal perdition, instead of diminishing the burden of the vessel—that is, instead of unburdening the soul of her sins—load her with a greater weight. Instead of flying from the danger of sin, they fearlessly continue to put themselves voluntarily into dangerous situations." (*The Sermons of St. Alphonsus Liguori*)

I like this analogy. Just as the people on board a ship in danger of sinking must throw their possessions overboard in order to lighten the ship's load and thus save their lives, so must we throw overboard everything in our lives that is threatening to drown us in a sea of sin and thereby save our souls. That process of taking every sinful influence in our lives and throwing it overboard starts with other people.

You know who those people are in your life and why they have to go. Cut them loose. Throw them all overboard.

Habitual sinners will be the first to go, along with those who are easily swayed by the opinions of others. If you don't end your relationship with them, and end it now, you'll risk being sucked down into their vortex of sin.

Look at the monks of old who retreated to the desert, to caves, or to any place where they could be alone. Part of the reason why they did that was to perform penance and atone for past sins, like Saint Mary of Egypt. But it was also to avoid the corrupting influence of other people.

It's a hundred times easier to avoid sin if you avoid other people. Add prayer and spiritual reading to the mix and you'll find avoiding sin to be a breeze.

Family Members Too

If you have family members who refuse to face facts, who insist on sinning and damning their souls to hell, then you really have no choice other than to cut them loose from your life. Failure to do so puts your own soul at risk of eternal damnation. Purge them or God will purge you.

Too harsh, you say? Heaven is not for wimps.

> Matthew 10:36-38: "And a man's foes shall be they of his own household. He that loveth father or

mother more than me is not worthy of me: and he that loveth son or daughter more than me is not worthy of me. And he that taketh not his cross, and followeth after me, is not worthy of me."

Now obviously here we're talking about people above the age of reason. For centuries, the Church has held the age of reason—the age when a child is capable of recognizing right from wrong and is thus capable of committing mortal sin—to be around seven-years-old.

However, that presupposes that the child has had a Christian education. How many children do you know today who are receiving a Christian education? Certainly not anyone who isn't being homeschooled, and of those that are being homeschooled, how many are being taught true Christian doctrine? The answer is almost none.

If you're sending your children to a private school in the belief that they are receiving a Christian education, I can assure you that they are not. There isn't a school or college anywhere in the world today teaching true Christianity and it's been that way for decades. The teachers and school officials at whatever school you're sending your children to can lie all they want, but I guarantee you they are not giving your children anything close to a true Christian education. How can they when the teachers and officials themselves don't know what true Christianity is?

Your children need to be taught right from wrong in order to go to Heaven. They need to be baptized as early as possible and taught true Christianity. They're not getting any of those things at school. So be patient with your children. However, adult family members who refuse to change and insist on traveling the road to perdition need to be purged from your life.

This is one of those uncomfortable truths that people don't want to hear. In fact, there are habitual sinners reading this right now whose heads are exploding with rage. That's because misery loves company, and no one is more miserable than an obstinate sinner.

When a sinner is left alone, they are forced to confront the reality of the life they're leading, an experience that is often too painful to bear. Add to that, the possibility of their own family abandoning them and they scream like banshees.

But what choice do you have? If a family member chooses to abandon God, then you, as someone who loves God, must abandon them.

Not only must we avoid contact with people and family members who are unrepentant sinners, we must also avoid contact with anyone who isn't a committed Christian.

Anyone in your life who belongs to a false, non-Christian religion or to no religion at all has to go. Don't keep them as friends. Don't buy their products. Don't partner with them in business. Don't associate with them on any level. Throw them all overboard.

> 2 Corinthians 6:14-15: "Be ye not unequally yoked together with unbelievers: for what fellowship hath righteousness with unrighteousness? And what communion hath light with darkness?"

The exception here is if you are trying to evangelize someone, to lead them away from their false religion and into the true Church of Jesus Christ. Other than that, you cannot afford to associate with anyone who is not a committed Christian. Doing so is forbidden and puts your soul at tremendous risk.

People of Bad Will

You're going to discover, to your utter dismay, that almost everyone you encounter in life, including your closest friends and family members, is a person of bad will.

A person of bad will is someone who obstinately refuses to face the truth. There are three primary reasons why so many people do that and all three reasons stem from pride.

The first reason why people of bad will refuse to face the truth is because they don't want to admit that what they believed previously is wrong. As I stated earlier, I've never had a problem with that, so it mystifies me why others do. But for most people their self-image, which is to say their pride, will not allow it. So they deny reality.

The second reason why people of bad will refuse to face the truth is closely related to the first. It's because they are more concerned with the approval of other people than they are with the approval of God.

Thus, when they encounter new information, a person of bad will doesn't ask, "Is this true?" They ask, "What will people think of me if I believe this is true?" And in almost every case, they will conform to the majority, no matter how ridiculous the position, in order to fit in with the herd.

The need to conform, to fit in with the herd and not to be different is so strong and so overpowering in people of bad will that it's as if they all got together and said, "Let's pretend to believe in something that doesn't make sense and isn't true, because it will unite us against those other people who believe in truth and reality."

That attitude has led to people of bad will being duped into believing the most ridiculous lies and absurdities coming from the Fake News media.

Their inability to recognize truth is a form of spiritual mental illness, and because they are more concerned with what others think of them, rather than with what God thinks of them, God allows them to be deluded by lies. Saint Paul describes such people here:

> 2 Thessalonians 2:10-12: "And with all deceivableness of unrighteousness in them that perish; because they received not the love of the truth, that they might be saved. And for this cause God shall send them strong delusion, that they should believe a lie: That they all might be damned who believed not the truth, but had pleasure in unrighteousness."

You might think it's cruel for God to send "strong delusion" to such people "that they should believe a lie," but the fact is if people of bad will were capable of recognizing truth, they wouldn't act any differently. As Saint Paul says, they take "pleasure in unrighteousness." Those last three words—"pleasure in unrighteousness"—contain the third reason why people of bad will refuse to face the truth.

Facing the truth requires a person to make changes in their life, changes which include giving up their sins, and most people just don't want to do that. They enjoy their sins and they'll fight like the devil to avoid giving them up.

In today's world, the so-called Information Age, nothing is hidden, and that's despite our living in the most censored society in all of history. Anyone who wants to know the truth can find it. Yet billions of people purposely avoid the truth in order to keep sinning. With that being the case, what *should* God do with them? What would *you* do?

Out of the mass of misguided humanity, you might find one person in a thousand who isn't a person of bad will, someone who is capable of self-reflection and original thought. That's if you're lucky. It will usually be a young person, someone in their teens or even younger, with an air of innocence about them; someone who hasn't been seduced by sin and beaten down by society.

On rare occasions, you will encounter an adult who isn't possessed of bad will. It will almost always be someone who is young at heart and keeps to themselves. But people like that are scarce; so scarce as to be practically non-existent. Most adults care more about worldly status and the opinions of others than they do about God.

> John 12:43 "For they loved the praise of men more than the praise of God."

People of bad will are as old as time. In Noah's day only eight people were saved. The rest drowned because they were people of bad will and hid from the truth. In the time of Lot only he and his family were saved. All the other inhabitants of Sodom were destroyed in a hail of fire and brimstone.

Those examples of Noah and Lot give you a pretty good idea of the number of people in the world today who possess bad will versus the number of people who don't.

Nothing has changed. Almost everyone in the world today is a person of bad will, just as they were in times past and just as they have been throughout all history.

To a person of bad will, facts and evidence are irrelevant and data doesn't matter. The only thing that counts is what others think of them. What they lack in discernment they make up for in their ability to be easily brainwashed and duped.

People of bad will refuse to listen to reason. That hasn't stopped them from having an opinion on everything, including and especially subjects of which they know nothing about. In fact, the less they know about a particular topic, the stronger their opinion on it is.

When faced with a topic they don't understand, the average person will admit as much with a simple, "I don't know." Not so, the person of bad will. There is nothing on earth which they claim not to know. Maybe they've read one book on a subject; maybe they've watched one video. Maybe they haven't done either of those things—it doesn't matter. In their mind they're an expert on it.

People of bad will are quick to criticize and condemn. Any time you put yourself out in the world—whether you write a book, make a video, post a comment, or engage in conversation—you immediately attract attention from people of bad will and draw the ire of imbeciles.

> "If you wish to lead a holy life, you must expect the ridicule and contempt of the wicked."—Saint Alphonsus Liguori, *Preparation for Death*

People of bad will are so heavily invested in the false beliefs that dictate their lives that they simply can't let go. Even if you prove to them that white is white and black is black, even if you show them concrete proof that their beliefs are built on lies and baseless conspiracy theories, even if you explain to them that a complete reversal of course is necessary in order to save their own soul, they still won't budge. They have literally lost the ability to process truthful information.

People of bad will are big-time television watchers. That shouldn't surprise you as people of bad will like being told what to think, rather than having to think for themselves. Television to them is a mental life preserver. Without it they wouldn't know what to think, what to believe, or how to act about anything. Asking a person of bad will to give up television is like asking a junkie to give up heroin.

Harboring Secret Sins

Not every person who sins is a person of bad will. But every person of bad will is a person who sins and someone who is harboring secret sins.

Take a close look at the people in your own life who are blind to the truth and you will see that this is so. Each and every one of them is harboring secret sins; sins that their denial of truth allows them to continue without remorse. And the more insistent they are at denying the truth, the deeper their sins go.

That they are on the road to hell is irrelevant to them. They either don't believe in hell or they belong to one of the two camps we talked about earlier—the "but I'm a nice person" camp or the faith alone camp.

Perhaps you're wondering whether a person of bad will can be changed into a person of good will. The answer is yes, they can, but it's rare. I've already told you that I'm a much different person now than I was growing up. But I also told you that I'm an exception. Almost everyone I know is the exact same now as they were on the day I met them.

Also, the change from bad will to good will has to come from within. You can't force it on someone else. In fact, trying to force a person of bad will into seeing the truth is almost impossible. You can send them article after article, video after video, book after book . . . none of it will matter.

They either won't look at the material you sent them, or they'll take only a cursory look at it before spiraling down into a vortex of cognitive dissonance.

So, yes, it is possible for a person of bad will to come to their senses and change. But it isn't likely. Almost everyone you know who is of bad will today, will be of bad will tomorrow, and the next day, and so on, until the day they finally die and find themselves in hell.

Remember, God knows everything, past, present and future. Some people weren't put here to evolve and seek His glory. Their purpose here is to show you what it looks like if you don't.

The Bible speaks eloquently and often about people of bad will:

> John 12:37: "But though he had done so many miracles before them, yet they believed not on him."

> Luke 16:31: "And he said unto him, If they hear not Moses and the prophets, neither will they be persuaded, though one rose from the dead."

> John 12:40: "He hath blinded their eyes, and hardened their heart; that they should not see with their eyes, nor understand with their heart, and be converted, and I should heal them."

Those Bible passages describe almost everyone I know. They probably describe almost everyone you know too.

You don't want to be a person of bad will for obvious reasons. Not only will it make you sad and miserable in this life, it will send you straight to hell in the next.

Your best bet in dealing with people of bad will is to avoid them completely. Don't associate with them. Don't engage them in conversation. Don't do business with them. Treat them like lepers. Failure to do so puts your own soul at risk of eternal damnation.

Is it truly necessary to go to that extreme? You tell me. Suppose someone informed you that they intended to douse their clothing with gasoline and set themselves on fire . . . would you spend time with that person?

Probably not.

What if you encountered such a person on the street, already soaked in gasoline and holding a lit match in their hand? Would you stand next to them?

Again, probably not.

Standing too close to such a person would put you at risk of being burned right along with them.

Well, what is the difference between someone who deliberately sets themself on fire in this world and someone who deliberately sets themself on fire in the next?

Because that's what almost everyone you meet and see in this world is doing. They are deliberately following a path that is leading them straight to hell. If you stand too close to such a person, if you spend time with them and ignore all of their warning signals, you put yourself at great risk of being sucked right along with them down to the bowels of hell.

The only intelligent way to deal with such a person—and remember, this includes almost everyone you now know and everyone you will encounter for the remainder of your life—is to avoid them completely.

Does this mean we have to become hermits? Yes, pretty much—but hermits in modern society. We don't have to live in a cave or seclude ourselves on a mountaintop. Although doing so would certainly earn one merits in Heaven. But we do need to avoid other people, both people we know personally and people we meet on social media.

Learn to Love Solitude

It's impossible to contemplate God and establish a relationship with Him when you're constantly surrounded by other people. It can only be done in the silence of solitude.

Spending time with other people increases the likelihood that you will be corrupted by their influence and end up burning in hell. Thus, one of the easiest ways to help ensure your salvation is to avoid the company of other people.

And since practically everyone you meet in life is in a state of mortal sin that means avoiding almost everyone.

Over half of the women you know personally or pass on the street or interact with in life have had abortions. They've literally murdered their own child, the most evil and disgusting act imaginable.

Of the women who haven't murdered their own child, a large segment of them support abortion and vote for pro-abort politicians in order to keep abortion legalized, which is also a grave sin. Almost none of these women have received the sacrament of confession.

What this means is that almost every woman you meet is in a state of mortal sin and on her way to hell. Do you really want to spend time with someone like that? Every second you do, increases the chances that you will join them in hell.

But let's not stop there, because it's the same with men. Over half of the men you know personally or pass on the street or interact with in life have impregnated women who went on to have an abortion.

The remaining men spend their time reading and watching pornography, getting drunk or high, and engaging in all manner of sin. Many of them are homosexual. Almost none of them have received the sacrament of confession.

In other words, almost every man you meet is also in a state of mortal sin and on their way to hell. And every second you spend with them increases the chances that you will join them in hell.

God is not found in or with other people. He can only be found in the quiet of solitude. To increase your odds of going to Heaven, you must practice the art of solitude.

Solitude is a sign of intelligence as the more you learn about life, the less you want to be around people.

Solitude includes removing ourselves from the presence of relatives, for as Saint Alphonsus said, "Relatives are very often the worst enemies of the sanctification of Christians."

Of course, if someone wants to climb the ladder of worldly success, they'll do the exact opposite of everything I've just said here.

They'll smile and ingratiate themselves with everyone they meet. They'll go out of their way to attend office parties and company functions. They'll conform to the herd on every issue and earn brownie points along the way. They'll achieve huge success in the world. That is, until the day they die and find themself cast into everlasting fire.

Charitable or Not Charitable?

There are those who say avoiding other people is being uncharitable. But let me point out a hidden benefit to doing so. When you dismiss someone from your life, they no longer hold any influence over you, which is good.

At the same time, when you dismiss someone from your life, you no longer hold any influence over *them*, and that can also be good. After all, how many times have you led others to sin? I know I have and I regret it painfully.

If I had avoided certain people, they'd have been much better off. They might have gone ahead and sinned anyway with someone else, but I have no way of knowing that. As it stands, I'm responsible for participating in sin with them. All I can do now is pray that God forgives us both.

When you look at it in those terms, avoiding other people might be the most charitable thing you could possibly do for someone else. You just might save someone's soul by avoiding them.

> "When one separates oneself from many friends and acquaintances as well as from distracting business in order to serve and praise God Our Lord, one gains no small merit before the Divine Majesty."—Saint Ignatius of Loyola, *The Spiritual Exercises*

Words of Hope, Meant Just for You

By refraining from sin, practicing daily and consistent prayer, and avoiding other people, you've taken huge strides on the road to Heaven. But we still have a ways to go. Remember, very few people are saved. If we wish to be among them, we have to follow their lead and do exactly what they did. And one thing they all did was to withdraw from the world.

We'll cover that in detail in the next chapter. For now, rest assured that you are well on your way to eternal paradise in Heaven.

> "If you knew how quick people would forget about you after your death, you will not seek in life to please anyone but God."—Saint John Chrysostom

Chapter Six

More Easy Ways to Lead a Virtuous Life

People aren't the only thing we need to purge from our lives in order to increase our chances of going to Heaven. We also need to purge places. If a particular place—a nightclub, a gym, a cubicle at work where the cute girl sits—causes you to experience temptation and engage in sin, stop going there.

Stay away from amusement parks, including that famous one you're thinking of right now. It's not a place of innocent childhood fun. The people who own and run that particular park are among the biggest pedophiles in the world.

Avoid public pools and beaches—they are cesspools of sin and temptation.

Turn down that party invitation. Say no to that dance. Don't visit a friend if you think doing so will lead you into temptation and sin.

Places to avoid can also consist of cities. Look at Las Vegas. It's not called Sin City for nothing. Avoid it like the plague.

There are cities in Asia and Europe—I won't mention their names—that tourists flock to in order to pay for prostitution. Don't even think about visiting them.

Books, Movies, Television, and Music

If you're serious about going to Heaven, then books, television, movies, and music all have to go.

When I say books, I mean romance novels; fantasy novels; any book featuring witches, werewolves, vampires, or demons; any book that includes sexual content or profane language; any book that espouses New Age philosophy or any form of religion outside of Christianity.

To play it safe and help ensure your salvation, political books and biographies of anyone who isn't a saint should also go. Basically, you're going to have to stop reading 100% of what's coming from traditional publishers and 99% of what's coming from the independents.

Too hard, you say? It's better for you to toss all of your trashy romance novels and never read another one than it is to be cast into hell for all eternity.

Better yet, instead of tossing them, burn them. Or at least rip the pages out before tossing them. That way no one who finds them will fall into sin by reading them.

Of course, books are only the tip of the iceberg. I recommend giving up anything and everything coming from the so-called entertainment industry. That means not only books, but also television, movies, and music. Television, movies, music, and traditional book publishing are not about entertainment. They're not even about money, although money plays a part. What they're about is turning society upside down by making the abnormal appear normal.

They do their dirty work by taking behavior that's sick and sinful and calling it normal. Then they glamourize it, help to legalize it, and present it as something desirable.

Television, movies, music, and traditional publishing represent everything that is wrong with the world today. They brainwash the masses by denouncing what's good and promoting what's bad. It's a sick and twisted agenda and it drives them relentlessly.

Take It from an Insider

I've produced and acted in movies and television. I can tell you firsthand that both industries are riddled with sin, and both are run and populated by the most despicable people on earth. You have no idea how bad the situation actually is.

The people who work in movies and television hold you, the viewer, in utter contempt. To them, you're garbage; literal human scum. If I told you the giddy delight they take in mocking you with fake news, woke programming, and insulting commercials and sitcoms, you would never watch movies or television again. That is, if you have self-esteem. If not, you'll keep watching.

The entertainment industry is rotting your brain with all of its lies and hypnotic programming. It's setting you up for failure. It's telling you to hate what's good and to love what's bad. It's telling you to hate your own race. It's telling you to hate yourself.

The situation wasn't quite so bad a few years ago when I was making movies—or maybe I just didn't notice—but it sure is now. If you're serious about saving your soul, then you simply can't afford to watch movies or television.

In fact, I would go so far as to call it a necessity and say that anyone who continues to watch movies or television is almost certain to end up in hell when they die.

That's not an exaggeration. A person who watches movies or television and refuses to stop is exposing themselves to a lifetime of lies and sinful programming that's purposely designed to corrupt their soul and send them to hell. I've never met anyone strong enough to resist that. In fact, I doubt that such an individual even exists.

Both movies and television were instrumental in helping to steal the 2020 presidential election. That makes everyone involved with both industries guilty of treason, a crime punishable by death—death by hanging.

Both movies and television conspired to push the virus hoax, which has now killed tens of millions of people worldwide and injured millions more.

Movies and television openly push homosexuality and trannyism, which includes the legal kidnapping and sexual mutilation of children. The Bible speaks very eloquently on the fate that awaits those who harm children. It says it would be better for them if a stone were tied around their neck and they were cast into the sea. These are the very people you're supporting every time you watch movies or television.

Continuing to support either of those industries is the very definition of aiding and abetting the enemy. I don't see how anyone who does that stands even the slightest chance of going to Heaven. It is simply inconceivable to me that God, who is all good, would allow such a person into Heaven.

If you're bristling at the thought of giving up movies and television in order to go to Heaven, how do you think I feel? I could be making movies right now, living on the beach in Malibu and enjoying all the perks of life. But when I realized how destructive the industry was, and how intrinsically evil the people running it were, I was faced with a choice. I could continue making movies and enjoy a life of fame, money, and unlimited sex—only to end up in hell. Or I could give it all up for God.

I chose the latter.

When I run into people from my movie days, they're aghast at the choice I made. But it comes down to priorities. They're chasing fame, money, and sex. I'm chasing Heaven. If you're chasing Heaven too, then I strongly suggest you remove movies and television from your life. Believe me, you won't regret it.

Purge All Pornography

While we're on the subject of movies and television, this is a good time to point out the need to purge all pornography from your life. If you're not currently reading or watching pornography, don't ever start. If you *are* currently reading or watching pornography, it's important to stop immediately and purge it all from your life. Pornography is disgusting and it leads to masturbation, a mortal sin that will send you straight to hell.

Not only that, but reading or watching pornography is a mortal sin in itself and will send you straight to hell.

You may not know this, but one of the main purposes of pornography is the destruction of Christianity. That's why it remains so rampant in our society.

Al Goldstein, a major producer of pornography, was asked why he did it. Goldstein said, "The only reason why Jews are in pornography is that we think Christ sucks. Catholicism sucks. Pornography thus becomes a way of defiling Christian culture."

In Goldstein's own words, you can see that the people pushing pornography do it because they hate God.

Can you imagine the immense sorrow you cause Jesus to suffer every time you read or watch pornography? Jesus died on the cross for you . . . you can't stop reading and watching pornography for Him?

If you're burning with lust and temptation, the solution is to pray more. A lot more. Saint Bruno said, "He hath a demon within him who persists in any grave sin." If that's the case with you, it's going to take some heavy-duty prayer to purge those demons.

Praying the Rosary is the best way to do that.

When you make the decision to purge yourself of pornography, and it's a decision you must make, be ready to suffer in the same way that anyone quitting an addiction suffers. The first step is to ask God for help.

Music is Even Worse

As bad as movies and television are, the music industry is even worse. And that's saying something. Did you know that Bob Dylan, Katy Perry, Kanye West, and others have all publicly admitted selling their souls to the devil? The video clips are widely available online.

Did you know that music industry insiders have revealed that the master recordings of rock songs are "consecrated" to demons before being released in order to invoke those same demons whenever the song is played?

John Todd was the first person to go public with that information back in the seventies. Todd's message was quickly suppressed and he was silenced. However, Shane Lynch of the band Boyzone recently confirmed everything that Todd warned us about.

Boyzone has six number-one singles and five number-one albums. It doesn't get much bigger than that, and industry insiders don't get much bigger than Lynch.

In a September 2023 interview with Megan Cornwell of Premier Christianity, Lynch said of the music industry, "It is (designed) to take you away from Christ, 100 percent. I've been in rooms—at the top of the top—where albums are prayed over demonically. Music is prayed over demonically that goes out to the radio stations, to the public. . . . Rituals, ceremonies, everything to give light to the devil, to Satan. It's a satanic music industry. Literally." This is exactly what John Todd told us.

Did you know that all of those rumors you heard about back-masking are true—that when you play popular music backwards you can hear the artists literally praising Satan? In some cases, you don't even have to play the music backwards; it comes out explicitly in the lyrics. There are dozens, possibly hundreds, of examples.

Did you know that rap music became popular through a deal between the music and prison industries? When the prison industry became privatized, they began looking for ways to increase the inmate population in order to increase their profits. Knowing how rap music that glorified drug use and gangsterism would lure young black men into crime and thereby increase the number of prison inmates, they offered the music industry a cut of their profits in exchange for promoting rap music.

The music industry took the deal and that's when rap went mainstream. For over thirty years now, countless young black men and young black women have languished in prison in order to line the pockets of those who conspired to make rap music popular.

While it's true that those who went to prison were guilty of crimes, would they have been inspired to commit those crimes if the music industry had not deliberately promoted rap music, knowing it would lead to criminal behavior?

And what about the innocent victims of those crimes— the people who were robbed and killed? They also suffered in order to enrich music and prison industry executives.

I've met dozens of A-list musical artists—the biggest names, the biggest bands, and the biggest sellers in the business—and I can tell you straight out that they are the most anti-God, anti-Christian people I have ever been associated with. In fact, I've never met anyone in the music industry who was a Christian, and I can say the same for the movie and television industries.

For the sake of your soul, you can't afford to have anything to do with movies, television, traditional book publishing, or music ever again. That goes for rock, country, rap, jazz, and pop music. The only music you can listen to, if you truly want to go to Heaven, is classical.

Sports Will Send You to Hell

The situation regarding mass "entertainment" has gotten so bad that you can't even watch sports anymore. Every sports league in the country holds Pride Nights. Every sports league in the country openly promotes homosexuality and trannyism (the legal kidnapping and sexual mutilation of children). Every sports league in the country came out in support of riots and looting during 2019-2020. Every sports league in the country pushed the virus hoax of 2020-2022.

Every sports league in the country is now onboard with ticketless stadium entry via facial recognition and cashless concession sales.

In other words, every sports league in the country openly promotes sin, crime, lawlessness, medical tyranny, sexual perversion, and the kidnapping and sexual mutilation of children. They all promote feminism and the feminization of men. They all promote everything that God is against. It's become impossible today to watch sports without sinning yourself.

In June of 2023, the Los Angeles Dodgers hosted a celebration by the Sisters of Perpetual Indulgence, a group of homosexual men dressed in drag as satanic nuns who openly mock God, Jesus, and the Crucifixion. It was akin to spitting in the face of God, an in-your-face insult to Christians everywhere, yet it really wasn't surprising. That's because the owners and commissioners of all four major sports leagues—football, baseball, basketball, and hockey—are Christ-hating men and women. There isn't a single Christian among them. If you support them in any way, whether by attending their games, buying their merchandise, or watching their games on television, what does that say about you? Do you honestly believe that God is going to let you into Heaven?

> Matthew 10:33 "But whosoever shall deny me before men, him will I also deny before my Father which is in Heaven."

But wait, there's more. Every sports league in the country schedules games on Sunday, which is a violation of the third Commandment to keep the Lord's Day holy.

If you doubt the seriousness of that, remember that Our Lady of La Salette said to the two young seers in France that God was dishonored and angry by people working on Sunday.

In fact, Our Lady was crying when she said that. That's how distressing it was for her. Yet every sports league in the country deliberately schedules games on Sunday, an open violation of God's third Commandment.

One can make the claim that by watching or attending the games they're not actually working on Sundays, but what about the people who are? The players and coaches, the security personnel, the parking lot attendants, the people selling popcorn and beer . . . they're working. And anyone who watches or attends the games is part of that. If they weren't watching, those other people wouldn't be working.

This is another example of gambling with your soul. If you err on the side of caution and avoid all professional sports and it turns out you're wrong—that there's nothing sinful about watching or attending the games—then you haven't lost anything. If you die in a state of grace, you'll still go to Heaven.

On the other hand, if you reject the notion that it's a sin to support an industry that schedules games on Sunday and that openly promotes homosexuality and the kidnapping and sexual mutilation of children, and you continue to attend or watch the games and it turns out you're wrong—that it *is* a sin to support such an industry—you're doomed. You could end up burning in hell for all eternity.

Which approach is safer? Which approach is smarter?

I'll admit giving up sports was a tough one for me. I'm one of the top-five football handicappers in the country. Giving up sports is costing me thousands of dollars. But just like I gave up movies and acting, I don't really have a choice. It's either give up sports or suffer the consequences, and those consequences could include spending eternity in hell.

The only possible exception to this—and I say "possible," because I don't know if God will accept it—is someone vacationing in the Gray Rock Hotel who watches sports on television as a temporary escape from their surroundings. But that's it. Anyone on the outside who continues to support professional sports is literally playing with fire.

As a child must one day put away its toys, adults need to stop wearing professional sports jerseys and stop watching the games. Every dollar spent on a jersey or attending a game is another dollar lining the pockets of the very people who openly mock God and support the kidnapping and sexual mutilation of children.

It's the same with movies, television, music, and traditional book publishing. If you want to go to Heaven, you can't have anything to do with any of them ever again.

The need to give up so many apparent pleasures of life is one of those painful truths that people of bad will don't want to hear. But I pledged to give it to you straight when I set out to write this book. And so I am.

We're all adults here. We have a responsibility to face the truth and acknowledge it, even and especially when we don't like what the truth reveals.

As for people of bad will, if they haven't thrown this book across the room yet, they will when they read the point I'm about to make next.

Purity is the Best Policy

What does dressing immodestly, buying or selling on Sunday, charging interest on loans, practicing Yoga, studying your horoscope, voting for pro-abortion politicians, and reading romance novels and Harry Potter books all have in common?

The answer is they all describe behavior that has become so normalized in modern society that almost no one realizes how horribly sinful it is. If you tell someone engaged in any of those activities that what they are doing is a sin, you will be met with a flurry of indignation. And none of those actions will invite more outraged indignation at being called a sin than dressing immodestly.

To realize just how widespread the sin of immodest dress actually is, consider that in the Book of Isaiah, God refers to a woman's bare legs as "nakedness" and "shame."

> Isaiah 47: 1-3: "Come down, and sit in the dust, O virgin daughter of Babylon, sit on the ground: there is no throne, O daughter of the Chaldeans: for thou shalt no more be called tender and delicate.
>
> "Take the millstones and grind meal: uncover thy locks, make bare the leg, uncover the thigh, pass over the rivers.
>
> "Thy nakedness shall be uncovered, yea, thy shame shall be seen: I will take vengeance, and I will not meet thee as a man."

That's pretty intense. According to the Bible, to uncover the thigh, which is to show any part of the leg above the knee, is a great sin. And yet today we have both men and women displaying their legs, shoulders, midriffs, and more. Such behavior is actually encouraged.

Of course, people today—most notably atheists and Christ-haters—will point out that we no longer live in ancient times; that such changes in dress represent "progress." While it's true that we no longer live in antiquity, does man's so-called progress mean that God has also changed? Is God, who created time itself, somehow behind the times?

Jacinta Marto, one of the three seers of Fatima, was visited several times by Our Lady and told many things. Shortly before she died in 1920, Jacinta revealed to Mother Godinho, a nun in Lisbon who ran an orphanage where Jacinta stayed before being admitted to the hospital, "My dear Mother, the sins that bring most souls to hell are the sins of the flesh. Certain fashions are going to be introduced which will offend Our Lord very much. Those who serve God should not follow these fashions. The Church has no fashions: Our Lord is always the same." (*Blessed Jacinta Marto of Fatima* by Msgr. Joseph A. Cirrincione, page 54)

So much for God changing with the times.

NOTE: Despite the misleading title of the book where Jacinta's quote was taken, she is neither Blessed, Venerable, nor a Saint. The same with her brother Francisco. That's because only a valid pope can proclaim someone Blessed, Venerable, or a Saint; and the Congregation of Saints, the agency of the Church responsible for overseeing all things related to the causes of saints, must be composed of valid cardinals and bishops. Since the implementation of Vatican

II in the 1960s, the Church has had neither of those things. It hasn't had a valid pope nor valid cardinals or bishops.

You can prove this to yourself quite easily by referencing the Papal Bull of Pope Paul IV in which he declared in 1559 that a heretic cannot be a validly elected pope. You can also consult the Catholic Encyclopedia of 1914, Volume 11, page 456, which states: "Of course, the election of a heretic, schismatic, or female (as Pope) would be null and void." You can look up the teachings of the doctors of the Church which emphatically declare that a pope who commits the sin of heresy is automatically excommunicated from the Church and ceases to be the pope. (More on this in a later chapter.)

Thus, we can see that neither John Paul II, who called Jacinta and Francisco both Venerable and Blessed, nor Francis, who called them Saints, are valid popes as both have committed multiple acts of heresy.

That's not to say that Jacinta and Francisco don't deserve to be saints, only that they have never been named Venerable, Blessed, or a Saint by a valid pope.

This is yet another of those truths that people of bad will don't want to hear, but truth is truth, and facts are facts.

Back to the subject of immodest dress, Padre Pio was enraged by the sin of immodest dress and refused to hear the confession of any woman who wasn't wearing a skirt that extended at least eight inches below the knee. He chased them out of the confessional, calling them "clowns," and shouting, "Out! Out! Out!" (*Padre Pio: A Catholic Priest Who Worked Miracles and Bore the Wounds of Jesus Christ on His Body* by Brother Michael Dimond.)

So along with removing from our life people of bad will, sinful people, un-Christian people, places of sin, movies, television, music, professional sports, and almost all books, we must also refrain from the sin of immodest dress. That pertains to both guys and girls. Neither sex can wear anything that fits tight or is even slightly revealing. That is, of course, if you really want to go to Heaven.

Withdraw from the World

What all of this boils down to is you have to withdraw from the world. You have to purge from your life almost everything that other people are concerned with.

And guess what? That happens to be the third commonality among everyone that we know with a high degree of certainty is now in Heaven. They all withdrew from the world and they all encouraged others to do the same.

What's more, the world they faced was tame compared to the world we live in today. The majority of them didn't have television, movies, or satanic music to contend with.

They weren't faced with rampant homosexuality and the sexual mutilation of children. They *did* have trashy books, as we do today, and they spoke out harshly against them.

They had the theater, which they condemned. They condemned dancing. They condemned sinful sporting events.

Saint John Chrysostom vigorously condemned the chariot races which took place in his day, as well as the theater: "Flee, therefore, I beg of you, the spectacles of Satan and the harmful sights of the racecourse." (*On Wealth and Poverty* by Saint John Chrysostom, page 140)

If any of the people that we know with a high degree of certainty are now in Heaven could see the world as it exists today, they would recoil in horror.

Imagine Padre Pio watching ten minutes of modern day television. He would take a sledgehammer to it and forbid every member of his parish from ever watching television.

If we desire to go to Heaven, we must do the same. We must condemn the world and withdraw from it completely. We really have no choice.

Too hard, you say?

It is and it isn't.

If you really want to go to Heaven, it's not hard at all.

If you're attached to the things of this world, then it's very hard, excruciatingly so. But consider the alternative.

We're at the point in time where you're either with God or you're with the devil. I know you're with God, because you're reading this book. But you're an exception. Most people aren't with God. Baseball, beer, and pornography mean more to them than going to Heaven. They'd rather read romance novels, wear short skirts, and vote for pro-abort politicians than praise and honor Jesus Christ. So into the lake of fire they go.

Don't blame me, I'm merely the messenger. I want to see everyone in Heaven, especially you. I'm detailing in the pages of this book what everyone that we now know is in Heaven did in order to get there. Consider it a road map. I intend to follow that map every step of the way, no matter what the rest of the world thinks, says, or does. I urge you to do the same.

Lose the World or Lose Your Soul

Withdrawing from the world is an absolute necessity for anyone who desires to go to Heaven. You really have no choice. As long as you remain in the world, it's going to be almost impossible for you to stop sinning.

Remember the words of Saint Anselm: "If thou wouldst be certain of being in the number of the elect, strive to be one of the few, not one of the many. And if thou wouldst be sure of thy salvation, strive to be among the fewest of the few."

To be among the fewest of the few means you must do the exact opposite of what everyone else is doing. While everyone else is "following their dreams" and pursuing worldly "success," you must do the opposite. You must withdraw from the world.

Every time you flee from the occasion of sin, it's a crown of glory earned for you in Heaven.

Every wicked invitation you turn down is a feather in your cap before God.

Every sinful person you release from your life earns you another song from the Heavenly choir of angels.

If that's not enough for you and if you think you have it tough by giving up a handful of vain pleasures look at what the Apostles went through:

Saint Matthew was beheaded in Egypt.

Saint Andrew was crucified in Greece.

Saint Philip was crucified in Asia, Minor.

Saint Bartholomew was skinned alive and crucified.

Saint Paul was beheaded.

Saint Peter was crucified upside down.

Saint Matthias was burned alive.

Saint Thomas was pierced to death.

Saint Mark was dragged to death.

Saint Simon was sawn in half.

Saint Jude was crucified.

Saint James, son of Zebedee, was beheaded.

Saint James, son of Alpheus, was stoned and clubbed to death.

Saint Stephen was stoned to death.

And you're complaining because you can't watch television.

The Bible urges us to withdraw from the world.

> James 4:4: "Know ye not that the friendship of the world is enmity with God? Whosoever therefore will be a friend of the world is the enemy of God."

> 1 John 2:15: "Love not the world, neither the things that are in the world. If any man love the world, the love of the Father is not in him."

The saints have all urged us to withdraw from the world. Everyone that we know with a high degree of certainty is now in Heaven has urged us to withdraw from the world. I think it's pretty clear that if we want to go to Heaven then we too must withdraw from the world. We must follow the example laid down by everyone that we know is now in Heaven.

The Final Step

We've seen that the first commonality among everyone that we now know is in Heaven is the avoidance of sin. We've seen that the second commonality among them is daily and consistent prayer. And we've seen that the third commonality among them is detachment from the world.

There's one more commonality among everyone that we know with a high degree of certainty is in Heaven that you need to be aware of; one more thing that they all did and that the vast majority of people never do.

For some people, this final step will be the hardest of the four to accept; for others it will be a piece of cake. If you find it difficult, then I urge you to read through to the end of the book before passing judgment. You can find out what this final step is in the very next chapter.

Words of Hope, Meant Just for You

If avoiding other people and withdrawing from the world appears daunting to you, it doesn't have to be, because you really won't be missing much. Everything on television and at the movies is trash. Streaming services are worse. Video games are a waste of time. Professional sports are a woke joke. Almost all books being published today are garbage.

Music is literally satanic.

Sex is overrated. It provides a momentary thrill—I'll give you that. But then what? If there's no love involved, and sometimes even when there is, then as soon as it's finished, you're left with a hollow feeling and your mind immediately moves on to something else. And if the sex you engaged in was outside of marriage, you're overwhelmed with shame. For a moment's pleasure, you've punched your one-way ticket to hell.

Eliminating all of the above from your life doesn't leave a whole lot. You'll have to find your fun elsewhere, in the laughter of children, the beauty of nature, or a playful pet.

As you engage in solitude and quiet contemplation, you'll find that the pleasures of the world mean less and less to you. You'll find your peace in prayer and your joy in God. And you'll come to know that the closer a soul draws to God, the simpler life becomes.

Here's something else to ponder. We are all cosmically connected. By that I mean, what each of us does in our own life reverberates and influences everyone else in the world, both the people we know and the people we don't know. Your decision to withdraw from the world is going to have a profound effect on others in ways you could never imagine. Put that in your pipe and smoke it.

"He, then, who wishes to be saved must forsake not only all sin, but the occasions of sin—that is, the companions, the house, the connections which lead to sin."—Saint Alphonsus Ligouri, *Preparation for Death*

Chapter Seven

God Wants You Here

What is the fourth and final commonality among everyone that we know with a high degree of certainty is now in Heaven? Before I tell you, let me say that we could have listed this commonality first among the four as it is absolutely necessary for anyone who desires to go to Heaven. However, the reason I chose to list this one last instead of first is because it is certain to enrage people of bad will.

Not that the first three commonalities haven't already done so. But this last commonality trumps those other three by far. It is absolutely guaranteed to send people of bad will into a tailspin of spittle-flying outrage. If I had listed it first, many of them would not have read this far, and by reading this far some of them may have actually begun the process of changing from a person of bad will to a person of good will, as rare as those cases are.

They might still reject the book at this point, but what they've read in the previous chapters will remain with them.

At a future point, when their mind is ready to accept the truth, they might return.

For some of you this will be the most difficult chapter in the book to embrace. However, it is essential that you do so, because without it you simply cannot enter Heaven. So let's lay out the evidence and let the chips fall where they may. Are you ready?

Every single person that we know with a high degree of certainty is now in Heaven happened to be . . . a traditional Catholic. They were all baptized Catholic and they all died within the Catholic Church. At the same time, we have zero evidence that anyone who died outside of the Catholic Church is now in Heaven. Therefore, in order to be saved and go to Heaven, you must become a traditional Catholic.

I can hear the groans and howls of indignation from some of you right now, along with whiny complaints that the Catholic Church is not Biblical. The reality is the exact opposite. The Catholic Church is entirely Biblical. In fact, it's the only religion in the world whose every teaching is confirmed in the Bible. No other religion can say that.

Penance, purgatory, confession, Holy Communion—it's all in the Bible. From the appointment of Peter as the first pope of the Catholic Church (Matthew 16:18-19), to confessing one's sins to a validly ordained priest (John 20:23), everything the Catholic Church teaches is confirmed by the Bible, including the Hail Mary prayer (Luke 1:28 and 1:42) and the Immaculate Heart of Mary (Luke 2:35).

You can prove this to yourself quite easily by picking up a Bible and reading it. (For some reason, those who are most opposed to the Catholic Church never seem to want to read the Bible.) You can also read the book *The Bible Proves the Teachings of the Catholic Church* by Brother Peter Dimond which contains detailed information on this subject.

If you don't already know that everything the Catholic Church teaches is confirmed by the Bible, then you've been misled. There's no shame in that. We've all been misled. The shame lies in being too proud to admit it. And when it comes to the Catholic Church almost everyone has been misled.

There is more confusion, more misinformation, and more downright stupidity regarding the Catholic Church—what it is and what it isn't—than any other issue affecting the world today.

If you recall what we discussed earlier about people of bad will having opinions on subjects which they know nothing about, the Catholic Church is a prime example of that. I doubt if more than one person in fifty thousand actually knows what the Catholic Church is. Yet the remaining 49,999 all have an opinion on it. The situation is so absurd that even among the 1.2 billion people in the world who consider themselves Catholic almost none of them know what the Catholic Church actually is.

So what is the Catholic Church?

Let's start with what it isn't. The Catholic Church is not the clown show currently taking place in the Vatican under antipope Francis. It's not the series of wicked antipopes that have falsely laid claim to the papacy since the late 1950s.

It's not what's being taught in today's "Catholic" schools, hospitals, and charities.

It's not a pagan religion instituted by Constantine.

It's not a front for the Illuminati, nor a front for the Jesuits, whose Black Pope secretly controls the world—a position of such incomprehensible stupidity that it boggles the mind.

It's not any of those things.

What is the Catholic Church?

The Catholic Church is the same now as it's ever been; the same Church that was founded by Jesus Christ in approximately 33 A.D.

Jesus said, in John 14:6, "I am the way, the truth, and the life: no man cometh unto the Father, but by me."

That's an unambiguous statement. It leaves no room or opportunity for interpretation. Jesus says, "no man cometh unto the Father," and by that He means no man enters Heaven, "but by me."

Earlier in the same book of John, 10:16, Jesus says, "And other sheep I have, which are not of this fold: them also I must bring, and they shall hear my voice; and there shall be one fold and one shepherd."

That's another unambiguous statement. Jesus says, "there shall be one fold and one shepherd." In other words, there will be one Church and one leader of that Church.

Then in Matthew 16: 18-19, Jesus says, "And I say also unto thee, That thou art Peter, and upon this rock I will build my church; and the gates of hell shall not prevail against it. And I will give unto thee the keys of the kingdom of heaven:

and whatsoever thou shalt bind on earth shall be bound in heaven: and whatsoever thou shalt loose on earth shall be loosed in heaven."

There we have more unambiguous statements by Jesus, establishing His Church and appointing Peter as the first pope. Thus, we can see in language that even a child can understand that the only way to Heaven is through Jesus by way of His Church, and that His Church was established in 33 A.D., with Peter as the first pope.

Now notice Jesus' use of the word "church," which is singular. He did not say "churches," which is plural. In other words, there is only one church—not two, not two hundred, not two thousand—only one. So put your thinking cap on and reason this one out.

If there is only one true Church of Jesus Christ, and if it was established in approximately 33 A.D., then which church is it? It can't be any Protestant church, because none of them were invented until after the Protestant Revolution in 1520.

Martin Luther, who instigated the Protestant Revolution, was a Catholic until 1520 when he invented his own religion. Before Luther there were no Protestant religions.

The Church of England did not exist until 1534 when King Henry VIII invented it.

The Baptist Church did not exist until 1606 when John Smyth invented it.

And so on down the line. Every Protestant denomination in existence was invented after the year 1520. Therefore, from a simple process of elimination, we can see that none of them are the true Church of Jesus Christ.

If we take the Bible at its word and accept that Jesus started His one true Church around the year 33 A.D., then the only church it could possibly be is the Catholic Church, because the Catholic Church is the only Christian religion that was in existence at the time. From the founding of Jesus' church in approximately 33 A.D., up until the year 1520, to be a Christian meant to be a Catholic, period.

Saint Ignatius of Antioch, a disciple of the Apostle John, wrote in his letter to the Smyrnaeans in approximately 100 A.D., "Just as where Jesus Christ is, there is the Catholic Church."

So you can see that even the church fathers recognized the one true Church of Jesus Christ as the Catholic Church right from the beginning.

Remember, there were no Baptists, Methodists, Lutherans, Evangelicals, or anyone else calling themselves Christian until after the year 1520. They simply did not exist. The only Christians on earth were Catholics.

That means anyone who considers themself a Protestant is following a religion made by man. That's the reality.

If you don't believe me, ask any Protestant preacher when his church was founded. If he's honest, he'll tell you.

If he's dishonest (and I'm betting he is), he'll lie and say it was founded at the time of Christ in 33 A.D. In which case you can then ask why his particular denomination didn't have any "churches" or "pastors" in existence prior to 1520. Why did they all suddenly pop up after the Protestant Revolution in the 1500s? He'll likely lie again and say something about the "spirit of the church."

When you finally pin him down to admitting that his denomination was founded by a man sometime after the year 1520, ask him how he can justify belonging to a church that wasn't founded by Jesus Christ. At that point, your conversation will be terminated.

The situation is the same for anyone who calls themself a non-denominational Christian. Such a person is rootless and following a religion or spiritual path of their own making. They are outside of the true Church of Jesus Christ.

To add more fuel to the fire, consider this: Anyone who believes that the Catholic Church is not the true Church of Jesus Christ must also believe that from the time Jesus founded His church in 33 A.D. and appointed Peter as its first pope, up until the year 1520, there were no Christians anywhere on earth. After all, there were no Baptists, Methodists, Lutherans, Evangelicals, or anyone else calling themselves Christian until after the year 1520 A.D.

So anyone who believes that the Catholic Church is not the true Church of Jesus Christ must also believe that Christianity did not exist for 1,500 years.

And if that's the case, then for 1,500 years everyone who lived and died, including all of the saints and martyrs and all of the early Christians who were fed to the lions went straight to hell because they were all outside of Jesus' true Church.

Doesn't that seem a little farfetched to you?

Do you really think that Jesus would establish His Church, send His disciples out to preach the gospel far and wide, but then wait 1,500 years for His true Church to be recognized?

To believe that is a mockery of Jesus' promise to Peter that the gates of hell would not prevail against His church, because to say that it took until 1520 A.D., or later, for Jesus' true Church to be recognized presupposes that hell did prevail— for 1,500 years.

The True Church of Jesus Christ

The false belief that the Catholic Church is not the true Church of Jesus Christ is the primary reason why people avoid it. It's a sad situation because if those same people knew the truth they would readily embrace the Catholic Church. After all, who wouldn't want to align themselves with the true Church of Jesus Christ?

During the reign of Christian Europe prior to 1520 everyone did know the truth and they did embrace the Catholic Church. That's when Europe flourished. The Catholic Church literally built Western Civilization. Today, since abandoning Christianity, Europe is a shambles, with America not far behind.

Further confirmation that the Catholic Church is the true Church of Jesus Christ comes from the many fruits it has borne, through its missions, its art, and its miracles.

Catholic missionaries have evangelized non-Christians all over the earth, saving countless souls from eternal damnation. No other religion has done that.

The art and architecture of the Catholic Church has uplifted suffering humanity and beautified Europe for centuries. No other religion has done that.

Most telling of all, the Catholic Church is the recipient of countless miracles that defy the laws of nature, physics, gravity, and even reality itself. No other religion has that.

If it's Heaven you seek, don't discount the only religion in the world with such a long history of documented miracles. By documented, I mean scientifically investigated by experts both in and out of the Church and proven to be of supernatural origin.

From the Shroud of Turin (the burial cloth of Jesus Christ), to the tilma of Guadalupe (a supernatural imprint of the Mother of Jesus), to the Miracle of the Sun (witnessed by over 70,000 people), to the uncorrupt bodies of saints and seers (bodies which refuse to decompose after death), the Catholic Church has it all. All of the other religions in the world combined do not have a single documented miracle among them. The Catholic Church has thousands.

Let's look briefly at one aspect of the miracles associated with the Catholic Church—resurrecting the dead. Starting with Jesus Christ Himself, the Catholic Church, and only the Catholic Church, has raised the dead. Saint Peter and Saint Paul both raised people from the dead. So did Saint Benedict, Saint Anthony, Saint Bernard, Saint John Bosco, Saint Hilary, and many other Catholic saints.

Saint Vincent Ferrer raised over twenty people from the dead, and Saint Patrick, for whom the holiday is named, raised over thirty people from the dead.

All of those cases of resurrection were investigated by both Catholic and non-Catholic sources. All of them were deemed authentic miracles. Meanwhile, no member of a non-Catholic religion has ever raised a single person from the dead; certainly no Protestant preacher has ever done it. Isn't it time you joined the winning side?

If it's God's love you desire, consider carefully a religion whose churches, hospitals, schools, and missions have done more good for more people than any other organization in the history of the world.

Don't be in a rush to dismiss a religion that has saved Christianity and all of Western Civilization from destruction countless times. If not for the Catholic Church, the entire world today would be speaking Arabic and practicing Islam. In fact, you would likely have never been born if it wasn't for the heroic bravery of the Catholic Church.

As recently as 1683, militant Moslems were at the gates of Vienna, threatening to overrun all of Europe, and on the verge of victory, before their invasion was repelled by the Polish King Jan Sobieski in the most epic cavalry charge in all of history—his 20,000 Catholic horsemen against an army of 143,000 Islamic invaders. Had Sobieski failed, all of Europe would have fallen. The triumphant king and his men attended Mass the morning before the battle and afterwards they ascribed their victory to God.

For centuries, the Catholic Church has been the only power on earth strong enough to stand up to the evils of Communism and it remains so today.

Without the Catholic Church the entire world would fall into a dark abyss and we're seeing that take place today right before our eyes as Western nations have abandoned Christianity and are now paying the price. Europe has fallen.

Australia and New Zealand have fallen. Mexico has fallen. Canada has fallen. The United States has fallen. The world is on the brink of a total eclipse.

Finally, don't forget that the Catholic Church gave us the Bible. Without the tireless efforts put forth by dedicated Catholic Monks over the centuries, copying the Bible manuscripts by hand, the entire New Testament would not exist.

The Final Step on the Road to Heaven

Now that we've established what the Catholic Church is—the true Church of Jesus Christ—there's another piece of the puzzle we have to look at. It's an issue of immense importance and one whose mere mention is enough to send people of bad will into spastic rage. That's because even among those who know that holding the Catholic Faith is necessary for salvation, there exists immense confusion over what that Faith actually is.

The confusion stems from the Vatican II Council that took place in the 1960s. At that time, an entirely new religion was created. Just as Martin Luther invented his own religion in 1520, antipope Paul VI invented a new religion in the 1960s.

Even worse, Paul VI called his new religion Catholic and managed to convince countless followers that this new religion was an improvement over the traditional Catholic Church. Since then, billions of people have been duped into believing that this new religion that came into being under

Paul VI is the actual Catholic Church. Nothing could be further from the truth.

It's a frightening subject and reminiscent of the famous quote by former FBI director J. Edgar Hoover:

> "The individual is handicapped by coming face-to-face with a conspiracy so monstrous he cannot believe it exists. The American mind simply has not come to a realization of the evil which has been introduced into our midst. It rejects even the assumption that human creatures could espouse a philosophy which must ultimately destroy all that is good and decent."

Since Hoover uttered those words in August of 1956, the situation has only gotten worse. In 1956, the enemy lay concealed, like a snake in the grass, quietly plotting and carrying out its objectives. It was very hard then for the average person to spot the Communist subversion and takeover of the country that was occurring.

Today nothing is concealed. The enemy is blatantly out in the open and the fruits of Paul VI's new religion are there for everyone to see. So let's examine the situation. And as we have done throughout this book, let us do it with a preponderance of facts and evidence toward which nobody can offer a shred of rebuttal in any form. Fasten your seat belt and hold on tight. People of bad will are going to have their heads exploding all over the next chapter.

Words of Hope, Meant Just for You

God wants you in the Catholic Church—the *real* Catholic Church. You won't go to Heaven without it. Now that you understand that, it's a simple process of converting to the True Faith. But before we cover the steps to convert, it's in your best interest to read the next chapter so you can be sure that you are converting to the *real* Catholic Church and not to the counterfeit church invented by Paul VI.

In the meantime, know this: you're almost there. And by "there," I mean Heaven. By avoiding sin, praying every day, withdrawing from the world, and embracing the traditional Catholic Church, you are following the same path followed by everyone that we now know is in Heaven.

Stay on that same course and your success is guaranteed.

You will be going to Heaven, and I can't wait to see you there.

> "There is indeed one universal Church of the faithful, outside of which nobody is saved."—Pope Innocent III, *Fourth Lateran Council*

Chapter Eight

God *Doesn't* Want You Here

We saw in the last chapter that one reason why people avoid the Catholic Church is due to a false belief that it is not the true Church of Jesus Christ. No one has ever told them the truth that the Catholic Church *is* the true Church of Jesus Christ, established in 33 A.D., and that God has reserved salvation only for those who are baptized by water in the Catholic Church. As a result, billions of souls are now in hell and billions more are following in their footsteps.

Even worse, billions of other souls are now in hell, with more right behind them, because they are following a facsimile of the Catholic Church and not the real thing. They are either unaware or unwilling to admit that a counterfeit church has usurped both the Vatican and the Church's physical structures and has been impersonating the Catholic Church since the 1960s.

Have you ever seen a counterfeit twenty dollar bill? At first glance, the bill looks real. It's only upon closer inspection that you notice the subtle differences; the telltale signs that what you hold in your hand is phony and not the real thing. Once spotted, however, the fakery appears so obvious that you wonder how you were ever fooled to begin with. That is the situation today with the Catholic Church.

What people around the world today believe to be the Catholic Church is not the Catholic Church at all. It is a counterfeit church; a new religion that is not Catholic, but pagan to its core, and one that is leading billions of souls to hell.

Just like a phony twenty dollar bill, the counterfeit church appears real. Its members occupy the same buildings and physical structures. They wear the same vestments and recite prayers that closely resemble the old ones.

To someone not paying attention everything looks and sounds exactly the same. It's only upon closer inspection that the deception becomes obvious and, once spotted, cannot be denied. The Catholic Church has been infiltrated and subverted from within.

That doesn't mean the Catholic Church is vanquished. Jesus promised that would never happen when He appointed Peter the first pope and said, "And I say also unto thee, That thou art Peter, and upon this rock I will build my church; and the gates of hell shall not prevail against it." (Matthew 16:18)

The Catholic Church remains alive today, but only through the efforts of a small handful of faithful followers. It does not exist in any of the churches, schools, hospitals, charities, or other organizations that call themselves

Catholic; or in Rome which has become, in the words of Our Lady of La Salette, "The seat of the Antichrist."

When the average person, who doesn't have a clue what's going on, hears about the infiltration and subversion of the Church, they immediately deny it by citing the words of Jesus: "and the gates of hell shall not prevail against it."

What they fail to understand is that the Communist infiltration and subversion of the Church doesn't mean the real Church no longer exists. The subversion and takeover of the Church's physical structures and the survival of the true Catholic Church is not an "either-or" proposition. Both can exist simultaneously. And that is exactly where we are.

The Catholic Church still exists and it always will, just as Jesus promised it would. However, its existence is not dependent upon the number of its members.

Theoretically, the Church could be reduced to only one faithful follower and it would still exist. You alone—yes, you—could be the only traditional Catholic left in the world and the Church would still exist.

Here's an analogy to help better explain the situation.

At the time of this writing (September 2023), we have a man calling himself Joe Biden occupying a sound stage that's designed to look like the White House and claiming to be president.

Millions of low-IQ Americans, along with the entire mainstream media refer to him as the president, only he's not the president and never will be.

That doesn't mean the office of the presidency has ceased to exist. It hasn't. All it means is that an impostor is claiming to be president and a large number of people have been duped into believing it.

The situation in the Catholic Church with current antipope Francis, along with his predecessors going back to John XXIII, is no different. They occupy the Church's physical structures, they wear the vestments, and they claim to represent the Catholic Church. Only they don't. They represent a counterfeit church. And just like the man calling himself Joe Biden is not the president and never will be, the man born Jorge Bergoglio and calling himself Pope Francis is not the pope and never will be.

The similarities between the infiltration and subversion of the country and the infiltration and subversion of the Church are remarkable. In the same way that the stolen election of 2020 allowed "Joe Biden" and his handlers to claim the presidency, the implementation of Vatican II in the 1960s has allowed a series of antipopes and their handlers to claim they represent the Catholic Church. In both cases, people who have never studied the issue go along with it, because they don't know any better.

Here's another analogy. Suppose you had a neighbor named John Smith, and suppose you kidnapped him and moved your cousin into John Smith's house. Your cousin could then claim he was John Smith, and he could point to the fact that he's now living in John Smith's house and wearing his clothes to prove his case. If he was clever, he could convince the neighbors and legal authorities that he was John Smith. But none of those things would make him John Smith. He would forever be an impostor.

That's the situation with the Catholic Church today. Usurpers have taken over the Church's buildings and physical structures, they've donned Church's clothes and vestments, they've done their best to convince over a billion naïve followers that they actually are the Catholic Church, only they are NOT the Catholic Church and never will be.

Once you understand that, everything else suddenly becomes crystal clear. And you quickly recognize another reason why so many people today reject the Catholic Church. They do so because they believe the Church is a cesspool of sin and debauchery, littered with Communists and child molesters, and professing a false religion. Well, based on what they're seeing, they appear to be right.

What's being presented to the world as the Catholic Church *is* a cesspool of sin and debauchery, littered with Communists and child molesters, all of them professing a false religion. Only that's not the Catholic Church. It's a counterfeit church. And remember, that doesn't mean the real Catholic Church has vanished or ceased to exist.

The deception we are witnessing runs very deep. Literally billions of souls have gone to hell since 1968, because they remained in the counterfeit church, thinking it was the real Catholic Church.

Today, billions of more souls are on the road to hell for the very same reason. No one has told them that what they think is the Catholic Church is actually a counterfeit church, preaching a false religion and damning souls to hell.

The Communist infiltration and subversion of the Catholic Church was a long time coming. It's a plot that took centuries of planning and culminated with the Second Vatican Council in the 1960s. At that time, the Catholic Mass was changed from the traditional Latin Mass to an invalid and non-Catholic Protestant service, and the Traditional Ordination Rite for priests was also changed, rendering it invalid. Accompanying these changes has been a series of wicked antipopes all falsely claiming to be the pope.

This is the Great Apostasy that was prophesied in the last chapter of the Bible and foretold by Our Lady of La Salette when she said, "Rome will lose the faith and become the seat of the Antichrist." It's also the message of the Third Secret of Fatima which was never released to the public.

Anyone who gasps and says, "That could never happen!" is an idiot. It already has happened. We're living through it.

The Communist Subversion of the Church

How does someone infiltrate an organization like the Catholic Church? The answer is simple, and it's the same way you infiltrate any organization, you put your own people inside it.

Manning Johnson was a Communist agent who left the Party and wrote a book about his experiences called *Color, Communism and Common Sense*. In 1953, Johnson testified to the House Committee on Un-American Activities about the massive Communist infiltration of the Church:

> "Communists discovered that the destruction of religion could proceed much faster through

infiltration of the Church by Communist agents operating within the Church itself. . . .

"In the earliest stages it was determined that with only small forces available it would be necessary to concentrate Communist agents in the seminaries and divinity schools. The practical conclusion, drawn by the Red leaders was that these institutions would make it possible for a small Communist minority to influence the ideology of future clergymen in the paths most conducive to Communist purposes.

"The plan was to make the seminaries the neck of a funnel through which thousands of potential clergymen would issue forth, carrying with them, in varying degrees, an ideology . . . which would aid in neutralizing the anti-Communist character of the Church.

"This policy was successful beyond even Communist expectations. The combination of Communist clergymen, clergymen with a pro-Communist ideology, plus thousands of clergymen who were sold the principle of considering causes as progressive, within 20 years, furnished the Soviet apparatus with a machine which was used as a religious cover for the overall Communist operation ranging from immediate demands to actually furnishing aid in espionage and outright treason."

Manning Johnson was talking about the 1930s and 1940s. That's how far back the current subversion goes.

Bella Dodd

Bella Dodd was a 21-year member of the Communist Party USA who used her Communist connections to become the head of the New York State Teachers' Union (some things never change).

Dodd wrote about her experiences in the book *School of Darkness*. Like Manning Johnson, she also testified before the House Committee on Un-American Activities and spoke of the mass Communist infiltration of the country's teachers' unions throughout New York and the rest of the country.

Dodd was baptized Catholic as a child. After she left the Communist Party, she returned to the Church, confessed her sins, and went on a lecture tour. She is reported to have said at one of her public lectures, "In the 1930s, we put eleven hundred men into the priesthood in order to destroy the Church from within. . . . Right now they are in the highest places, and they are working to bring about change in order that the Catholic Church will no longer be effective against communism."

Dodd repeatedly said that the Catholic Church is the only religion truly feared by the Communist Party, and the only force capable of stopping it. That was almost a hundred years ago. Multiply Bella Dodd and Manning Johnson by dozens of other Communist agents around the world, each one training scores of men to enter the Catholic Church in order to subvert it from within, add a century of time for them to do their dirty work, and what do you get?

You get a counterfeit church that has abandoned the Holy Sacrifice of the Mass and replaced it with a Protestant service; a church whose "bishops" and "priests" routinely rape and molest children; a church led by a long series of heretical, non-Catholic antipopes dating back to late 1950s; a church that has completely abandoned Catholic teaching and dogma.

Christian Rakovsky and the Unknown Light

In 1938, at the same time that Bella Dodd, Manning Johnson, and others were training thousands of men to infiltrate and destroy the Catholic Church from within, Christian Rakovsky, a Freemason and one of the founders of Soviet Bolshevism, was arrested and interrogated by the all-seeing Stalinist Secret Police (NKVD).

Rakovsky admitted at his interrogation that the Catholic Church was Communism's #1 enemy and therefore must be destroyed. He then convinced the Soviets to make a pact with Germany for a double invasion of Poland as a pretext for England, France, and the United States to declare war on Germany in order to further Communism in Europe.

Rakovsky gave his interrogator three reasons to do this:

1) To destroy Germany for printing their own money and to prevent their example from spreading to other nations. According to Rakovsky, this was Germany's cardinal sin; the primary reason why they were targeted for destruction.

2) To stamp out Germany's nationalistic spirit and prevent it from spreading to other countries.

3) To weaken and destroy the Catholic Church.

Here are Rakovsky's own words from his tape-recorded interrogation reprinted in the book *Red Symphony* by Dr. J. Landowsky:

"Hitler, this uneducated and elementary man, has restored thanks to his natural intuition and even against the technical opinion of Schacht, an economic system of a very dangerous kind . . . he took over for himself the privilege of manufacturing money . . . he has by means of magic, as it were, radically eliminated unemployment among more than seven million technicians and workers.

"Are you capable of imagining what would have come of this system if it had infected a number of other states . . . This is very serious. Much more so than all the external and cruel factors in National Socialism . . . There is only one solution—war.

"We have yet another reason, a religious one. Communism cannot be the victor if it will not have suppressed the still living Christianity. History speaks very clearly about this: the permanent revolution required centuries in order to achieve its first partial victory by means of the creation of the first split in Christendom. Christianity is our only real enemy."

In return for helping to create a pretext for the Allies to attack Germany, Rakovsky, on behalf of his employers, promised the Soviets half of Europe at the conclusion of the war. When his interrogators expressed skepticism, Rakovsky advised them to contact Joseph Davies, the U.S. Ambassador in Moscow at the time to confirm everything he'd just told them. The rest is history.

Germany and Russia both invaded Poland—Germany to rescue its own citizens who were being raped, mutilated, and murdered by Polish terrorists in the Danzig Corridor, and Russia to seize territory—and then England and France ignored Russia and declared war on Germany.

It's worth noting that Rakovsky admitted in his interview that these same enemies of the Catholic Church had a hand in duping Martin Luther and engineering the Protestant Revolution.

It's also worth noting that Rakovsky's interrogation began just after midnight in the early morning hour of January 26, 1938, at the same time that the skies of Europe were illuminated by an unknown light.

Our Lady of Fatima told the young seers twenty years earlier that this unknown light would be a sign from Heaven that God intended to punish the world for its crimes by means of war, hunger, and the persecution of the Church and the Holy Father.

The unknown light that inflamed the skies of Europe was visible on the night of January 25, 1938 from 6:30 to 9:30 p.m. In Moscow time, where Rakovsky's interrogation took place, the time was 9:30 p.m. to 12:30 a.m. As this sign from Heaven illuminated the skies of Europe, the interrogation of Christian Rakovsky and the plans to start World War II were just getting underway.

The Catholic Gazette

In February of 1936, the London edition of the *Catholic Gazette,* an official Catholic organ, published an article about the Freemasonic infiltration of the Church.

The article contained the minutes of several Freemason meetings in which the plans for the subversion and takeover of the Church were discussed. Here are some quotes:

"We still have a long way to go before we can overthrow our main opponent: the Catholic Church. We must always bear in mind that the Catholic Church is the only institution which has stood, and which will, as long as it remains in existence, stand in our way.

"We have induced some of our children to join the Catholic body, with the explicit intimation that they should work in a still more efficient way for the disintegration of the Catholic Church, by creating scandals within her.

"We can boast of being the creators of the Reformation! We are grateful to Protestants for their loyalty to our wishes, although most of them are, in the sincerity of their faith, unaware of their loyalty to us. We are grateful to them for the wonderful help they are giving us in our fight against the stronghold of Christian Civilization . . .

"Let us therefore encourage in a still more violent way the hatred of the world against the Catholic

Church . . . Let us, above all, make it impossible for Christians outside the Catholic Church to be reunited with that Church, or for non-Christians to join the Church, otherwise the greatest obstruction to our domination will be strengthened and all our work undone."

Once again, we see a frank acknowledgement that the Catholic Church is the number one enemy of the forces of evil. We also see confirmation of Rakovsky's claim, that these same enemies of the Church were instrumental in duping Martin Luther and instigating the Protestant Revolution, an event that has condemned literally billions of souls to hell over the last 500 years.

The Church Today

We've just covered four impeccable sources, all from times past, confirming independently of each other a plot to destroy the Catholic Church.

They describe the situation as it was occurring *then*. You don't have to imagine how bad things are *today*. All you have to do is observe what has occurred and what is presently occurring: "Catholic" schools flying the rainbow flag and teaching sex initiation; child molestation and sex scandals in parishes all across the globe; "bishops" embracing sodomy and pushing homosexuality on children; "nuns" coming out as lesbians and feminists, and promoting abortion; antipopes denying the existence of hell, celebrating pagan religions and declaring that followers of false religions can be saved; and it just goes on and on.

None of this represents the Catholic Church. It is the work of the counterfeit church pretending to be Catholic.

The Second Vatican Council 1962 to 1965

The key turning point in the creation of the counterfeit church was Vatican II, whose documents contain over 200 heresies. Here's a baker's dozen of the various heresies contained in those documents.

Sanctification and truth are found outside the Church.

Outside the Church there is remission of sin.

People can be saved outside the Catholic Church.

Christians should promote the morals of other religions.

God is the father of all people.

Interior gifts of the Holy Ghost exist outside the Church.

At Mass, the priest acts in the name of the entire holy people.

The true Sacred Scriptures exist outside the Catholic Church.

Ecumenism promotes justice and truth.

The State cannot forbid non-Catholic religions.

Jesus Christ was the first-born of many brothers.

Catholics respect those with different religious opinions.

Each person is bound by the authority of their own conscience.

Those are only a handful of the heresies professed at Vatican II. There are over 200 more where these thirteen came from. As bad as these heretical statements are, they represent only the tip of the iceberg of the damage that resulted from the Second Vatican Council. The worst acts to come were the creation of the New Mass and the changes to the rite of ordination for priests.

The New Mass is Not Catholic

The Catholic Church forbids any changes to the Traditional Latin Mass.

> "It shall be unlawful henceforth and forever throughout the Christian world to sing or to read Masses according to any formula other than this Missal published by us. . . . Should any venture to do so, let him understand that he will incur the wrath of Almighty God and of the blessed Apostles Peter and Paul."—Pope Saint Pius V, July 14, 1570, *Quo Primum Tempore*

Despite the gravity of sin involved in changing the Mass, as forewarned by Pope Saint Pius V, it didn't stop Paul VI from perpetuating the greatest crime ever committed outside of the Crucifixion—the replacement of the Traditional Latin Mass with the New Mass in 1969.

The New Mass was designed by six Protestant ministers, along with the assistance of "Cardinal" Annibale Bugnini, a freemason since 1963 and thus an enemy of the Church, in order to change the Mass from a recreation of Christ's sacrifice to a celebration of man. To accomplish that, over 700 Catholic orations were stripped, communion rails were abandoned, and communion was instructed to be given by hand to show that the Communion wafer was only ordinary bread and that the priest administering it was no longer a representative of Christ, but an ordinary person. That point was further emphasized by allowing Communion to be given by laypersons. Worst of all, the words of the consecration were changed.

These are the traditional words of the consecration: "For this is my body. For this is the chalice of my blood, of the new and eternal testament: The mystery of faith, which shall be shed for you and for many unto the remission of sins."

Those traditional words of the consecration were changed to this: "For this is my body. For this is the chalice of my blood, of the new and eternal testament. It shall be shed for you and for all so that sins may be forgiven."

As you can see, the words "the mystery of faith" were removed, and the words "which shall be shed for you and for many unto the remission of sins" were changed to "it shall be shed for you and for all so that sins may be forgiven."

Those changes may appear insignificant, but they are actually catastrophic. The words "the mystery of faith" signify Christ's presence in the Eucharist. Removing them indicates that Jesus is not present in the Eucharist.

Changing the words "which shall be shed for you and for many unto the remission of sins" to "it shall be shed for you and for all so that sins may be forgiven" completely changes the form and intention of the consecration.

Christ did not shed His blood for *all*. He shed His blood for the elect, the members of His Church. Here are His exact words at the Last Supper:

> Matthew 26:28: "For this is my blood of the new testament, which is shed for many for the remission of sins."

> Mark 14:24: "And he said unto them, This is my blood of the new testament, which is shed for many."

> Luke 22:20: "This cup is the new testament in my blood, which is shed for you."

Changing the words of the consecration to imply that Christ shed his blood for all is a deliberate falsification of what Jesus actually said. It implies that Jesus shed his blood for heretics, nonbelievers, unrepentant sinners, members of false religions, even Satanists.

This change in the form and intention of the consecration is not an accident. It was purposely designed that way by the freemason Bugnini and by the Protestant ministers who were tasked with creating the New Mass. It renders the consecration invalid, as confirmed by no less of an authority than Pope Saint Pius V.

> "Now if one were to remove, or change anything in the form of the consecration of the Body and Blood, and in that very change of words the wording would

fail to mean the same thing, he would not consecrate the sacrament."—Pope Saint Pius V, *De Defectibus*

"The words 'for you and for many' are used to distinguish the virtue of the Blood of Christ from its fruits: for the Blood of Our Savior is of sufficient value to save all men but its fruits are applied only to a certain number and not to all."—Saint Alphonsus Liguori, *Treatise on the Holy Eucharist*

"According to the Catechism of the Council of Trent the words 'for all' were specifically not used by Our Lord because they would give a false meaning."—Brother Michael Dimond and Brother Peter Dimond, *The Truth about What Really Happened to the Catholic Church after Vatican II*, page 107

What all this means is that the New Mass is invalid. It's not a Catholic Mass. It's a Protestant service pretending to be Catholic. And because the consecration is invalid, Jesus Christ is not present in the Eucharist.

Paul VI didn't just change the Catholic Mass, he obliterated it. Catholics must not attend the New Mass under penalty of mortal sin.

The New Rite of Ordination is Not Valid

At the same time that the invalid New Mass appeared, so did a change in the ordination rite for priests. Paul VI removed from the Traditional Rite of Ordination every duty administered to a priest that set him apart from a layperson.

The Traditional Rite of Ordination contained this prayer: "Theirs will be the task to change with blessing undefiled, for the service of thy people, bread and wine into the Body and Blood of Thy Son."

That prayer specifically grants to priests the power to consecrate the host and wine. In other words, it contains the essence of what occurs at Mass, which is Christ's presence in the Eucharist. That prayer was removed from the rite of ordination in 1968.

The Traditional Rite of Ordination contained this prayer: "Be pleased, Lord, to consecrate and sanctify these hands by the anointing, and our blessing. That whatsoever they bless may be blessed, and whatsoever they consecrate may be consecrated and sanctified in the name of Our Lord Jesus Christ."

That prayer grants to priests the power to bless and consecrate. It was removed in 1968.

The Traditional Rite of Ordination contained this prayer: "Receive the power to offer sacrifice to God, and to celebrate Mass, both for the living and the dead, in the name of our Lord."

That prayer grants to priests the power to celebrate Mass. It was removed from the rite of ordination in 1968.

The Traditional Rite of Ordination contained this prayer: "Receive the Holy Ghost. Whose sins you shall forgive, they are forgiven them; and whose sins you shall retain, they are retained."

That prayer grants to priests the power to forgive sins. It uses the same words that Jesus used in John 20: 22-23 when He granted to the Apostles the power to forgive sins through the sacrament of confession. That prayer was removed from the rite of ordination in 1968.

Can you understand the cataclysmic results of these changes to the rite of ordination for priests? It removed their power to bless, to consecrate the host and wine, to celebrate Mass, and to forgive sins. In other words, it removed every grace and power intended for them by Jesus Christ. It made priests no different than lay people and rendered the entire rite of ordination invalid.

Stop and consider the immense ramifications of that. It means that all "Masses" given and all confessions heard by "priests" ordained after 1968 are invalid. It means that billions, possibly trillions, of sins confessed to "priests" ordained after 1968 have not been absolved.

In other words, the person who did the confessing continued to carry their sins, even unto death and judgment. Imagine how many billions of souls are now condemned to hell because they thought they had confessed their sins to a valid priest, but didn't. It's the greatest swindle in the history of the world.

The rite for consecrating bishops was also changed, rendering it invalid. Thus, since the late 1960s, the Traditional Latin Mass has been replaced with an invalid and non-Catholic New Mass; while the ordination rite for priests and the consecration rite for bishops have both been altered, making each of them invalid.

If this is all new to you and you are not absolutely breathless by this point, you may want to check your pulse. Everything discussed here is irrefutable proof that Paul VI created a new religion and foisted that new religion onto the faithful under the guise of calling it Catholic.

About Those Wicked Antipopes

As you recall from an earlier chapter, it is the teaching of the Church that a heretic cannot be elected pope, nor retain the office of pope, and that anyone who commits the sin of heresy is automatically separated from the Church, whether they are a lay person, a bishop, or a pope.

That is Catholic dogma. To deny it is a mortal sin.

> "A pope who is a manifest heretic automatically ceases to be pope and head, just as he ceases automatically to be a Christian and a member of the Church."—Saint Robert Bellarmine, *De Romano Ponitface* II

> "In the case in which the pope would become a heretic, he would find himself, by that fact alone and without any other sentence separated from the Church. . . . He could not be a heretic and remain pope, because, since he is outside of the Church, he cannot possess the keys of the Church."—Saint Antonious

"It (the Holy Roman Church) firmly believes, confesses and preaches that no one outside the Catholic Church, not only pagans, but neither Jews nor heretics and schismatics, can become partakers of eternal life, but will go into eternal fire, which is prepared for the devil and his angels (Matthew 25:41), unless before the end they are united to the same life."—Pope Eugene IV, Papal Bull *Cantate Domino*, the Council of Florence, 1441

"Of course, the election of a heretic, schismatic, or female (as Pope) would be null and void."—*Catholic Encyclopedia*, 1914, Volume 11, page 456

"If ever at any time it shall appear that any Bishop, even if he be acting as an Archbishop, Patriarch, or Primate; or any Cardinal of the aforesaid Roman Church, or, as has already been mentioned, any legate or even the Roman Pontiff, prior to his promotion or elevation as Cardinal or Roman Pontiff, has deviated from the Catholic Faith or fallen into some heresy: the promotion or elevation, even if it shall have been uncontested and by the unanimous assent of all the Cardinals, shall be null, void, and worthless."—Pope Paul IV, Papal Bull *Cum ex Apostolatus Officio*, February 15, 1559

"By the heart we believe and by the mouth we confess the one Church, not of heretics, but the Holy

Roman, Catholic, and Apostolic Church outside of which we believe that no one is saved."—Pope Innocent III, *Eius exemplo*, December 18, 1208

We can clearly see that the Church declares all heretics to be outside of the Faith and unworthy of Heaven, and that anyone who commits the sin of heresy is automatically separated from the Church. Knowing that, let's take a look at some of the heresies committed by the men who claimed to be pope after Pius XII.

To list all of the heresies committed by these men would require a book 600 pages long. (In fact, someone has written that book, it's called *The Truth about What Really Happened to the Catholic Church after Vatican II* by Brother Michael Dimond and Brother Peter Dimond, and I strongly encourage you to read it.) We'll list only a handful of those heresies here, but enough to convince you that all of these men were notorious heretics and thereby separated from the Church.

John XXIII

John XXIII called the Second Vatican Council and began the formal process of creating a counterfeit church.

John XXIII was a Freemason, and therefore an enemy of the Church, as confirmed by Yves Marsaudon, himself a Freemason and author of the book *Ecumenism Viewed by a Traditional Freemason to Pope John XXIII and Pope Paul VI*.

John XXIII said that non-Christians could be called Christians, because of their "good deeds."

John XXIII referred to Jews as the Chosen People. He removed the phrase "perfidious Jews" from the Good Friday Liturgy in 1960, and composed a special prayer for the Jews which states: "Forgive us our unjustified condemnation of the Jews. Forgive us that by crucifying them we have crucified You for the second time."

John XXIII said non-Catholics are not separate from the Church.

John XXIII blessed the Muslim Shah of Iran.

John XXIII blessed members of false religions.

John XXIII said Christians can vote for Communists.

Paul VI

Paul VI replaced the Traditional Latin Mass with the invalid and non-Catholic New Mass.

Paul VI changed the Traditional Rite of Ordination for priests, rendering it invalid.

Paul VI created a new religion and called it Catholic.

Paul VI spoke repeatedly about holding esteem and respect for non-Catholic religions.

Paul VI called non-Christian religions "noble."

Paul VI praised the Hindu Shinto Temple.

Paul VI recommended birth control.

Paul VI praised the United Nations.

Paul VI frequently wore the same breastplate as the high priest Caiaphas, who ordered Jesus' arrest and crucifixion. It is the same vestment that is worn by High Priests in American Chapters of the Royal Arch of Freemasonry. Wearing it is an act of total apostasy.

John Paul I

John Paul I recommended birth control.

John Paul I praised the intentions of the Freemasons behind the French Revolution.

John Paul I said all the people of the world share the same "father."

John Paul I called Paul VI "a great pope."

John Paul II

John Paul II taught that non-Christian religions, including Wicca (Witchcraft) and Satanism were inspired by the Holy Ghost.

John Paul II repeatedly taught that man is God. The Bible says this is the sign of the antichrist.

John Paul II taught that those outside of the Catholic Church can be saved.

John Paul II taught that all men belong to the Catholic Church.

John Paul II prayed with Lutherans and gave a blessing to Lutherans.

John Paul II referred to Buddha as "Lord Buddha" and bowed before a statue of Buddha in a Buddhist temple.

John Paul II kissed the Koran.

John Paul II organized a World Day of Prayer for Peace attended by the leaders of dozens of false religions.

John Paul II invited Satanists to pray at the Vatican and removed or covered all crucifixes so they would not be seen.

John Paul II prayed with Satanists and participated in voodoo ceremonies.

John Paul II participated in Jewish services, an act of public apostasy.

John Paul II has been photographed numerous times making the 666 Eye of Horus sign, signaling to the world that he is a Freemason and thus an enemy of Jesus Christ and the Church.

Outside of Paul VI, antipope John Paul II is responsible for leading more souls to hell than anyone else who ever lived.

Benedict XVI

Benedict XVI taught that Catholics should not convert non-Catholics.

Benedict XVI attended Jewish services, an act of public apostasy.

Benedict XVI attended Islamic services and prayed in a Mosque.

Benedict XVI claimed that there were "pagan saints."

Benedict XVI claimed the Bible is based on "pagan creation accounts."

Benedict XVI wrote the forward to a book entitled *The Jewish People and Their Sacred Scriptures in the Christian*

Bible, in which the author claims that Jesus doesn't have to be seen as the Messiah.

Benedict XVI taught that Catholics should respect false, non-Catholic religions.

Francis

Francis teaches that Jesus will accept practicing homosexuals.

Francis teaches that people in a state of mortal sin may receive Communion.

Francis teaches that all men will be saved.

Francis attended Islamic services, an act of public apostasy.

Francis attended a Buddhist Temple, an act of public apostasy.

Francis teaches that Catholics should pray with non-Catholics.

Francis claimed that Martin Luther was "intelligent" and offered a "remedy for the Church."

Francis said, "Lutherans and Catholics and all Protestants are in agreement on the doctrine of justification."

Any of these heresies or acts of apostasy taken on its own is enough to expel someone from the Church. Yet here we have multiple acts of heresy, one on top of the other, and remember, this is only partial list of the sins these men committed while claiming to be pope. You can see just from these limited examples that none of these men are even remotely Catholic. They are wolves in sheep's clothing who deliberately led their followers to the depths of hell. And Francis is doing the same right now.

Despite such overwhelming evidence that none of these men are valid popes and that all of them have been excommunicated from the Church, countless people calling themselves Catholic refuse to acknowledge that simple truth. It's an issue that people of bad will have a really hard time wrapping their heads around. All they know is what they see on television and if it's not on the idiot box, then, by golly, it can't be true.

In actuality, all of the heresies committed by these antipopes *have* been on the idiot box, only people of bad will weren't paying attention. They were too busy watching porn.

Let's look again at antipope Francis. In addition to the heresies and acts of apostasy already listed, Francis recently toured Europe where he openly and actively promoted the Islamic invasion currently taking place there. It was all over the television news. Yet people of bad will somehow missed it.

In 2017, Francis presented pro-abortion activist Lilianne Ploumen with a medal of honor in the order of Saint Gregory the Great as a personal prize and confirmation of her work in promoting abortion. That was on the news too.

Ploumen is the founder and head of "She Decides," a pro-abortion organization that raised over $300 million in its first year. According to the "She Decides" website, their number one priority is: "Abortion rights for everyone, everywhere."

Just recently, in June of 2023, Francis invited Andres Serrano to a celebration at the Sistine Chapel. Serrano's 1987 photograph entitled *Immersion* features Jesus on a crucifix submerged in urine. When Francis and Serrano met, Francis smiled and gave his friend a thumbs-up, thus signifying his approval for Serrano's "art." That story was widely publicized on every news channel, yet people of bad will didn't care.

Pause and think about these three very public acts of apostasy that Francis engaged in. He openly pushed for the Islamic invasion of Europe, demanding European countries take in more invaders. He presented a religious medal of honor to a woman whose organization is dedicated to promoting and legalizing abortion, the most despicable crime imaginable. He invited Serrano to a celebration at the Vatican, and then rather than condemn the man, Francis smiled and flashed him a thumbs-up.

Yet billions of brainwashed people continue to accept Francis and his predecessors as valid popes.

Jesus said, "By their fruits you will know them." The fruits are there for all to see, but the willfully blind refuse to acknowledge them.

You could make the case that none of these antipopes were legitimate popes to begin with, since they all held heretical beliefs before they were elected. In the case of Francis, he was ordained after 1968 in the false rite of ordination and therefore he was never even a valid priest. That makes his entire papal election null and void

There's nothing controversial about any of this. Ask yourself, "Is it Catholic dogma that heretics are automatically separated from the Church and lose their positions of office?"

Yes, you've seen the evidence.

Have all of the men claiming to be pope after Pius XII committed multiple acts of heresy?

Yes, you've seen the examples, and, remember, those are only partial lists.

Have all of these men therefore been excommunicated from the Church and did they all cease being pope?

Absolutely. It is the teaching of the Church. And to deny the teaching of the Church is to commit the mortal sin of heresy.

> "After the reception of baptism, if anyone, retaining the name Christian pertinaciously denies or doubts something to be believed from the truth of the divine and Catholic Faith (such a one) is a heretic."—Canon 1325, 1917 *Code of Canon Law*

So there you have it. Case closed. John XXIII, Paul VI, John Paul I, John Paul II, and Benedict XVI are all burning in hell, with Francis soon to follow. Nothing controversial about it.

By the way, whenever you hear the word "controversial," it means that someone's power is being threatened. In this case, anyone who calls the excommunication of heretical antipopes "controversial" is doing so because either their power or someone else's power is being threatened. That's all it means, nothing more.

"For men are not bound or able to read hearts, but when they see that someone is a heretic by his external works, they judge him to be a heretic pure and simple, and condemn him as a heretic."—Saint Robert Bellarmine, *De Romano Pontifice*

Your Soul, Your Choice

There's no sitting on the fence with this issue. We have to choose individually whether to embrace the true Catholic Faith or to follow the herd into the fires of hell. Denial is not an option, and ignorance is no longer an excuse. What matters is how you choose to react to this information.

The first thing most people do when they hear these truths is run straight to their parish "priest." But guess what? If that "priest" wasn't ordained before 1968, then he's not a validly ordained priest. He's a layperson posing as a priest. And if he doesn't know the truth himself, how can he be expected to render a truthful answer?

Others come across this information and turn to the internet for confirmation. That's all well and good, but the majority of websites that call themselves Catholic aren't Catholic at all. They're Vatican II gatekeepers, designed to keep the clueless within the pen of the counterfeit church.

If you wish to research this topic further, here's where you should go: www.MostHolyFamilyMonastery.com

You should also read the book *The Truth about What Really Happened to the Catholic Church after Vatican II* by

Brother Michael Dimond and Brother Peter Dimond. It's over 600 pages of irrefutable proof that what almost everyone today thinks is the Catholic Church is nothing but a wicked counterfeit church.

For those who say God would never allow His Church to exist without a true pope, the Church has had over 42 antipopes in its 2,000 year history.

And as we mentioned earlier, the infiltration and subversion of the Church was prophesied in the Bible. Jesus tells us that "in the holy place" itself there will be "the abomination of desolation" (Matthew 24:15), and a deception so profound that, if it were possible, even the elect would be deceived (Matthew 24:24).

If you're reeling from this information, I can understand. When I first heard it, I was somewhat shocked myself. That is, until I actually researched it for myself. At that point it became crystal clear.

It might help you to understand how this massive deception was accomplished by studying the history of Communist propaganda. Anthony Malcolm Daniels, known by his pen name Theodore Dalrymple, is an expert on the subject and his words here are especially relevant:

> "In my study of Communist societies, I came to the conclusion that the purpose of 'progressive' propaganda is not to persuade or convince, not to inform—but to humiliate; and so the less it corresponds to reality the better. When people are forced to remain silent when they are being told the

most obvious lies, or even worse when they are forced to repeat the lies themselves, they lose their sense of probity. To assent to obvious lies is to become evil oneself. One's standing to resist anything is eroded. A society of emasculated liars is easy to control."

The purpose behind Vatican II wasn't only to dismantle and destroy the Church from within, it was also to humiliate and emasculate Catholic men. By accepting a weak, watered-down, non-Catholic religion, those men became weak, watered-down, and non-Catholic themselves.

That has led us to where we are now, which is a classic case of Stockholm syndrome. The hostages (those who remain inside the counterfeit church) have developed a psychological bond with their captors (those keeping them in the counterfeit church), and have turned against those who are trying to rescue them from sin (traditional Catholics).

Words of Hope, Meant Just for You

This was a long, but necessary chapter and I commend you for sticking it out. If you follow through on the advice in this book, and I strongly urge you to do so, then it is imperative for you to embrace the true Catholic Church and not the mockery of the Faith coming from the counterfeit church.

To become a disciple of Christ and a member of His one true Church, there are four steps to take. First, you must believe in the teachings of the true Catholic Church. Second, you must be baptized Catholic, if you are not already. Third, you must live the remainder of your life as a traditional Catholic. That includes never attending a non-Catholic service like the New Mass ever again, and receiving confession only from a validly ordained Catholic priest. Last but not least, you must recite the Profession of Catholic Faith (included in this chapter).

The first step is easy. You can buy a five dollar copy of the book *The Penny Catechism* and learn the basic teachings of the Church. The book is small and only 70 pages long, so you can read through it very quickly.

You can also learn all about the Catholic Church and its teachings by reading articles and watching videos on the website www.MostHolyFamilyMonastery.com and on their companion website www.VaticanCatholic.com.

Once you are onboard with all of the teachings of the Catholic Church, you must be baptized Catholic, if you are not already. That, too, is easy. Contact the websites above and ask if they can refer you to someone in your area to baptize you.

The next step is confession with a validly ordained Catholic priest. That's going to be tricky, because most priests ordained before 1968 are now dead. Still, search your area and you might be able to find one, perhaps in a retirement home.

Don't confess your sins to anyone ordained after 1968, because it won't be valid.

You can also confess to an Eastern Rite priest at an Eastern Rite church, as they have been ordained in the

Traditional Rite of Ordination. Look for a Byzantine Catholic Church or Ukrainian Catholic Church. Ask the priest if he has been ordained in the Eastern Rite. If so, then that priest is an option for confession.

Finding a valid priest for confession is going to take some effort on your part. In the meantime, recite a Perfect Act of Contrition. A Perfect Act of Contrition will absolve your sins.

If you have never been baptized before, then after your first baptism, you do not need to go to confession right away as your baptism will absolve all of your sins. Sooner or later though, you will almost certainly have to go to confession.

Once you become a traditional Catholic, you must have nothing to do with the non-Catholic counterfeit church ever again. That includes never attending the non-Catholic and invalid New Mass. Your only option for Mass is the Traditional Latin Mass said by a non-heretical priest ordained in the Traditional Rite of Ordination. As I type these words in September of 2023, there isn't any such Mass being said anywhere in the world that I am aware of.

Since there are no valid options for attending Mass you have no obligation to attend. Attending Mass on Sunday is only an obligation if the Church provides you with a Traditional Latin Mass said by a non-heretical, validly ordained Catholic priest within reasonable distance. Thus, you should stay home on Sunday.

Staying home on Sunday is not as extreme as some people make it out. When the missionaries went out to preach the gospel to the world, they were often alone in the wilderness for months or years at a time. They had nowhere to attend Mass and no one to hear their confession. For the former, they prayed the Rosary on Sunday. For the latter, they relied on the Perfect Act of Contrition. A Perfect Act of Contrition is said out of love for God and our grief for having offended Him.

If you were shipwrecked on an island, God wouldn't hold it against you for not going to Mass on Sunday, because there wouldn't be any Mass for you to attend. The situation today is no different. There are no validly ordained, non-heretical priests offering the Traditional Latin Mass anywhere in the world. Thus, your only option is to stay home.

On the plus side, if you're a non-practicing member of any religion, or if you belong to no religion at all, then converting to the traditional Catholic Church is the easiest thing in the world. There is no Mass for you to attend and that won't be changing anytime soon, if ever. So all you have to do is follow the teachings of the Church.

What else is required? You will have to detach from the world; to be in the world, but not of the world. You must also pray the Rosary and you must stop sinning. Basically, all the points we covered earlier.

Above all, you must be persistent. You must maintain the Catholic Faith without compromise while everyone else around you is sinning and damning themselves to hell. It's not an easy task, but certainly one you can accomplish.

If anyone questions your actions, consider the source. If the person you're communicating with claims that the sin of heresy does not automatically separate one from the Church, then they are committing heresy themselves by denying Catholic dogma, which puts them in a state of mortal sin. Therefore, they should not be listened to.

In fact, no one in a state of mortal sin should be listened to. That includes anyone outside of the traditional Catholic Church, as well as anyone who denies the basic teachings of the Church, such as the necessity for water baptism, the dogma that outside the Catholic Church there is no salvation, etc.

No matter how good intentioned such people may appear to be they have disqualified themselves from any truthful and intelligent conversation. They should not be listened to on any subject.

If you apply such criteria it's going to drastically limit the number of people that you can safely hold a conversation with. But everyone you do talk to is going to be well-informed, well-intentioned, and most likely in a state of grace and on their way to Heaven.

If you confine your conversations to those specific people you can't go wrong. Of course, you may not feel the need to talk to anyone. As long as you're avoiding sin, praying every day, not partaking in the pleasures of the world, and embracing the true Church of Jesus Christ, *you're on your way to Heaven.*

> "Whoever wills to be saved, before all things it is necessary that he holds the Catholic faith. Unless a person keeps this faith whole and undefiled, without

doubt he shall perish eternally."—Council Fathers, Council of Florence, 1431-1449 A.D.

Act of Contrition

Oh my God, I am heartily sorry for having offended Thee and I detest all my sins, because I dread the loss of Heaven and the pains of hell; but most of all because they offend Thee my God, who are all good and deserving of all my love. I firmly resolve, with the help of Thy grace, to confess my sins, to do penance, and to amend my life. Amen.

Profession of Catholic Faith

I (your name) with firm faith believe and profess each and every article contained in the symbol of faith which the holy Roman Church uses, namely:

I believe in one God, the Father almighty, maker of Heaven and earth, and of all things visible and invisible, and in one Lord Jesus Christ, the only-begotten Son of God, born of the Father before all ages; God from God, Light from light, true God from true God; begotten not made, of one substance (consubstantial) with the Father, through whom all things were made; who for us men and for our salvation came down from Heaven, and was made incarnate by the Holy Ghost of the Virgin Mary, and was made man.

He was crucified also for us under Pontius Pilate, died, and was buried; and He rose again the third day according to the Scriptures and ascended into Heaven; He sits at the right hand of the Father, and He shall come again in glory to judge the living and the dead, and of His kingdom there will be no end.

I believe in the Holy Ghost, the Lord, and giver of Life, who proceeds from the Father and the Son; who equally with the Father and the Son is adored and glorified; who spoke through the profits.

I believe there is one, holy, Catholic and apostolic Church.

I confess one baptism for the remission of sins; and I hope for the resurrection of the dead, and the life of the world to come. Amen.

I resolutely accept and embrace the apostolic and ecclesiastical traditions and the other practices and regulations of that same Church.

In like manner I accept Sacred Scripture according to the meaning which has been held by holy Mother Church and which she now holds. It is her prerogative to pass judgment on the true meaning and interpretation of Sacred Scripture. And I will never accept or interpret it in a manner different from the unanimous agreement of the Fathers.

I also acknowledge that there are truly and properly seven sacraments of the New Law, instituted by Jesus Christ our Lord, and that they are necessary for the salvation of the human race, although it is not necessary for each individual to receive them all.

I acknowledge that the seven sacraments are: Baptism, Confirmation, Eucharist, Penance, Extreme Unction, Holy Orders, and Matrimony; and that they confer grace; and that of the seven, Baptism, Confirmation, and Holy Orders cannot be repeated without committing a sacrilege.

I also accept and acknowledge the customary and approved rites of the Catholic Church in the solemn administration of these sacraments.

I embrace and accept each and every article on Original Sin and Justification declared and defined in the most holy Council of Trent.

I likewise profess that in Mass a true, proper, and propitiatory sacrifice is offered to God on behalf of the living and the dead, and that the Body and Blood together with the Soul and Divinity of our Lord Jesus Christ is truly, really and substantially present in the most holy Sacrament of the Eucharist, and that there is a change of the whole substance of the bread into the Body, and of the whole substance of the wine into the Blood; and this change the Catholic Church calls transubstantiation.

I also profess that the whole and entire Christ and a true Sacrament is received under each separate species.

I firmly hold that there is a purgatory, and that the souls detained there are helped by the prayers of the faithful.

I likewise hold that the saints reigning together with Christ should be honored and invoked, that they offer prayers to God on our behalf, and that their relics should be venerated.

I firmly assert that images of Christ, of the Mother of God ever Virgin, and of the other saints should be owned and kept, and that due honor and veneration should be given to them.

I affirm the power of indulgences was left in the keeping of the Church by Christ, and that the use of indulgences is very beneficial to Christians.

I acknowledge the holy, Catholic, and apostolic Roman Church as the mother and teacher of all churches and I unhesitatingly accept and profess all the doctrines (especially those concerning the primacy of the Roman Pontiff and his infallible teaching authority) handed down, defined and explained by the sacred canons and ecumenical Vatican Council I). And at the same time:

I condemn, reject, and anathematize everything that is contrary to those propositions, and all heresies without exception that have been condemned, rejected, and anathematized by the Church.

I (your name) promise, vow and swear that, with God's help, I shall most constantly hold and profess this true Catholic Faith, outside which no one can be saved and which I now freely profess and truly hold. With the help of God, I shall profess it whole and unblemished to my dying breath; and, to the best of my ability, I shall see to it that my subjects or those entrusted to me by virtue of my office hold it, teach it, and preach it. So help me God and His holy Gospel.

Chapter Nine

The Truth Shall Set You Free

In life there is only truth or the absence of it. In other words, there is either truth or untruth. Both cannot exist simultaneously.

One of the reasons why so many people today suffer from mental illness is because they don't like reality and want to change it. But man can't change reality. Only God can do that. When God performs a miracle, such as the imprint of Our Lady of Guadalupe on Juan Diego's cloak, or the miraculous image of Jesus on the Shroud of Turin, it's literally a shift in reality. God can do that. People can't.

In your personal quest for truth, you're going to discover that there are two competing realities that people choose to live in. The first is reality itself, where truth resides. This is a lonely reality. Less than 1% of the people in the world live in this version of reality.

The second reality is the Fake News/Wikipedia version of reality. This is the reality you see presented on television, talk radio, and almost the entire internet. People can just say anything, report anything, and call it true. And there's no shortage of low-IQ people who will believe it's true.

Some people call this second reality Clown World, which is an apt description. Whatever you call it, this second version of reality is a dangerous place that you do not want to inhabit. For that reason, I strongly encourage you to unplug from television, movies, music, traditional publishing, along with everything else the entertainment industry has to offer. When you unplug from those sources, you automatically unplug from a large segment of the second reality.

Roughly 75% of the people in the world reside in this second reality, where they consume a daily diet of fear-based delusions. Their reference point for reality isn't reality itself, but a constant barrage of lies put forth by those who control the media.

Between the first version of reality, inhabited by less than 1% of the population, and the second version of reality, where 75% of the population dwells, there is a no-man's land occupied by the remaining 24% of the population. Those who exist here are straddling the fence, with one leg in the first reality and one leg in the second.

On rare occasions, someone living in this no-man's land between reality itself and Clown World will experience a sudden shift in consciousness and make the leap fulltime into the first reality. Once they find themselves living in the first reality, they never leave. No one ever leaves the first reality. Sadly, no one ever leaves the second reality either. In this chapter, we're going to take a leap from the second reality to the first and address one of the most perfidious lies ever foisted upon humanity: the fraudulent claim that Jesus was a Jew, along with his parents Joseph and Mary, and all of the Apostles. Nothing could be further from the truth.

Now if you're like me—and if you've read this far into this book, you're probably more like me than you think—you can imagine the stuttering rage coming from people of bad will right now.

With no knowledge of the subject and without a minute's time spent in research, they are experiencing massive levels of cognitive dissonance. That's how deep the programming on this issue goes.

Because the lie that Jesus was a Jew is so deeply ingrained in so many people's minds, it requires a dose of intellectual dynamite in order to dislodge it—dynamite packed with facts, evidence and truth. So let's light the fuse and stand back!

The Word That Almost Never Was

Did you know that the word "Jew" does not appear in any Bible prior to the 1700s? In fact, the word "Jew" did not even exist until the year 1775. Imagine that. It means that for over 1,700 years, and even longer for the Old Testament, the word "Jew" was absent from the Bible. The word used in Latin was "Iudaeus," and the word used in Greek was "Ioudaios," which correctly translated into English is Judean, and it refers to the people living in Judea, not to any race or religion.

To call someone a Judean meant only that they resided in the area of Judea, in the same way that we refer to people living in America as Americans, or to people living in Canada as Canadians. It has absolutely no connection whatsoever to the people we know today as Jews.

What's more, Jesus was from the city of Nazareth in Galilee, as were all of the Apostles except for Judas, the traitor. Judas was from Judea and he is the only Apostle who could be referred to as a Judean, or as incorrectly translated today, a Jew.

In John 7:1 we read: "After these things Jesus walked in Galilee: for he would not walk in Jewry, because the Jews sought to kill him." That passage is from the incorrectly translated King James Bible, but it makes the point that there were no Judeans (incorrectly translated as Jews) in Galilee where Jesus was born and raised.

Some people, grasping at straws, will point to the words which Pontius Pilate had inscribed upon the Cross, words which have been incorrectly translated since the 18th century as "Jesus of Nazareth the King of the Jews." The actual words are "Jesus Nazarenus Rex Iudeorum," which when correctly translated into English are "Jesus the Nazarene Ruler of the Judeans."

We can see that with this inscription Pilate is confirming that Jesus is from Nazareth, not Judea. Pilate himself was the actual ruler of the Judeans. He was the administrator in Judea for the Roman Empire. And he did not want to crucify Jesus. But he was faced with an angry mob of bloodthirsty citizens crying, "Crucify him! Crucify him!"

According to all historical accounts, Pilate commanded a small garrison of men, armed with swords and spears. They were greatly outnumbered by the seething mob that was almost certainly armed as people carried swords then. Peter carried a sword and used it when Jesus was arrested. The multitude of men who arrested Jesus were armed with "swords and staves" (Matthew 26:47) and they were among the mob screaming at Pilate to crucify Jesus.

Before the invention of firearms, most military battles were won by the larger force. If the mob calling for Jesus' crucifixion had rioted, Pilate and his men would have been killed. So Pilate caved. He washed his hands of the whole affair. And because he was ashamed at his cowardice, he had those words put on the cross to mock Jesus' killers. The chief priests complained and asked him to change what he had written. But Pilate refused. He said, "What I have written I have written." (John 19:22)

So along with Pilate's inscription, there is no mention anywhere in the Bible that Jesus was a Jew.

And as Benjamin Freedman correctly points out in his book *Facts are Facts*, there were no people that we know today as Jews in Judea at the time that Jesus lived.

> "In the time of Pontius Pilate in history there was no religious, racial or national group in Judea known as 'Jews' nor had there been any group so identified anywhere else in the world prior to that time."—Benjamin Freedman, *Facts are Facts*, page 14

In the same way that the word "Jew" does not appear in any Bible prior to the 1700s (it only appeared after non-Catholic translators began writing their own Bibles), the word "Judaism" also does not appear. The religion known today as Judaism is derived from Pharisaism, a religious practice based on the Talmud. The Pharisees crucified Jesus.

When one realizes that Jesus was not a Jew, it becomes clear that Christianity did not evolve from Judaism. It was derived from Mosaism, the old law. Thus, the term "Judeo-Christian" is an oxymoron. There is nothing similar between Judaism and Christianity. Nothing at all.

When Jesus confronted the Pharisees, who practiced the religion known today as Judaism, he called them the spawn of Satan. Literally. That's what Jesus thinks about the religion we know today as Judaism. See for yourself:

> John 8:44: "Ye are of your father the devil, and the lusts of your father ye will do. He was a murderer from the beginning, and abode not in the truth, because there is no truth in him."

Jesus also called them liars and refuted their false claim of being ancestors of Abraham.

> John 8:39: "They answered and said unto him, Abraham is our father. Jesus saith unto them, If ye were Abraham's children, ye would do the works of Abraham."

Not only that, but the Pharisees admitted as much.

> John 8:33: "They answered him, we be Abraham's seed, and were never in bondage to any man."

If they were never in bondage, then they can't possibly be the Israelites of the Bible who were taken in captivity.

Which brings up another point: nowhere in the Bible does it say that Abraham was a Jew. Or that Moses was a Jew. Or that Noah was a Jew. Or that Jacob was a Jew. It says they were Israelites or Hebrews, not Jews.

The same with Jesus. He was not a Jew, nor of the Jewish faith. He was an Israelite. As were His parents Mary and Joseph, along with all of the Apostles except Judas, and all of the great names we recognize from the Old Testament. They were Israelites, not Jews.

People who have never studied this issue become confused at that. They believe because the Jewish state of Israel calls itself Israel, that the people we know today as Jews, as well as the Jewish people now living in Israel have an ancestral connection to the Israelites of the Bible. The truth is no such connection exists. Prominent Jewish scholars admit so themselves.

> "Strictly speaking it is incorrect to call an ancient Israelite a Jew or to call a contemporary Jew an Israelite or a Hebrew." —*1980 Jewish Almanac*

"Jews began to call themselves Hebrews and Israelites in 1860."—Judaica Encyclopedia 1971

"The return from Babylon and the adoption of the Babylonian Talmud marks the end of Hebrewism and the beginning of Judaism."—Rabbi Stephen Wise, President of the American Jewish Congress and the World Jewish Congress.

"This is not an uncommon impression and one finds it sometimes among Jews as well as Christians—that Judaism is the religion of the Hebrew Bible. It is of course a fallacious impression."—Ben Zion Bokser, *Judaism and the Christian Predicament*, page 59

"It was only in comparatively recent times, after the Jews became familiar with modern Christian literature, that they began to name their religion Judaism."—Rabbi Adolph Moses, *Yahvism, and Other Discourses*, page 1

The Jewish scholar Arthur Koestler in his highly praised and meticulously researched book *The Thirteenth Tribe* documents how the people we know today as Jews are not descendants of the ancient Israelites, but of the Khazars from Turkey, who converted to Judaism under King Bulan in the 8th century.

Every reputable historian of the past two hundred years agrees with Koestler.

Now that you know the facts, you can see that to allege that Jesus was a Jew or a follower of Judaism is simply laughable.

Actually, it's not laughable it's tragic, because the belief that Jesus was a Jew is responsible for sending countless souls to hell. For one thing, it prevents potential converts from embracing the true Church of Jesus Christ, because they foolishly believe that Jesus was a Jew and that the Catholic Church comes from Judaism.

For another, it leads millions of gullible "Christians" into celebrating Jewish holidays, visiting Jewish shrines, attending Jewish weddings and funerals, and even to partaking in Jewish services, all of which are condemned by the Church.

Finally, it pollutes the entire message of Christianity, which is the exact opposite of Judaism.

> "Jesus abhorred and denounced the form of religious worship practiced in Judea in His lifetime and which is known and practiced today under its new name 'Judaism.' That religious belief was then known as 'Pharisaism.' . . . Catholicism and so-called 'Judaism' are at the opposite extremes of the spiritual spectrum."—Benjamin Freedman, *Facts are Facts*

> "For Christianity did not believe in Judaism (Pharisaism), but Judaism in Christianity."—Saint Ignatius of Antioch, *Letter to the Magnesians*, approximately 100 A.D.

What you've just learned in this chapter is something very few people know. I didn't know it myself until just a few years ago. It was never taught to me in school or when I was growing up. Thankfully, there are courageous individuals researching and documenting this kind of information.

If you'd like to know more about this subject, the aforementioned book *Facts are Facts* by Benjamin Freedman is a good place to start. Freedman was a Jew who converted to the Catholic Faith and saved his soul. Jewish converts to the true Faith are often zealous promoters of the truth. Freedman was no exception.

Words of Hope, Meant Just for You

With each passing page of this book, you're drawing closer and closer to God. Don't be surprised if little "miracles" pop up along the way. They have for me.

At a Farmer's Market in Hollywood, I bought a small pendant featuring Our Lady of Guadalupe and put it around my neck. An hour later I was at the subway station, waiting for my train, and an elderly man commented on it.

"That's from Juan Diego, isn't it?" he said.

"Yes," I replied. "Do you know the story?"

He knew all about the miraculous image imprinted on Juan Diego's cloak. We talked about it until my train arrived. It was only later that I realized it was dark on the subway platform and he was sitting six feet to my side. He couldn't possibly have seen the tiny pendant I was wearing. Yet he did. How was that possible? (You can see that same pendant in my photo on the back cover of this book.)

Another time I was instant messaging a girl at a job, telling her all about Our Lady of Fatima and the Miracle of the Sun. I copied a lengthy article about the event from the website www.VaticanCatholic.com and sent it to her. Not five seconds passed before I received a chat from a customer.

Now you've probably seen or used customer chats before. They appear on numerous websites and allow you to instantly communicate with someone from the company whose website you're on. In our case, virtually every chat we received was from someone asking about a price on a product or the status of an order. In the four years I worked there, a period in which I saw literally thousands of those chats no one ever began one by stating their name. Not once. But this one did.

It said, "This is Mary."

And remember that took place less than five seconds after I sent information to a coworker about Mary's appearance at Fatima and the Miracle of the Sun.

Then there was the time I spotted an unusual-looking girl on a bus. The way she was dressed and the way she wore her hair, she looked to me like she had stepped out of the past. I remember thinking, she's from another era.

Later that day, I opened a library book that I had never read before, a book about saints. In the photo section in the middle of the book was an old black and white photo from 1892 of Saint Therese of Lisieux when she was nineteen-years-old, holding a sword and dressed like Joan of Arc for a play at her convent. That picture in the book was the same girl I saw on the bus, the girl who had stepped out of time.

Now, were any of these incidents actual signs from Heaven? That I cannot say. All I can do is relay the information and let you decide. However, the Bible does tell us that we will have contact with Heavenly visitors:

Hebrews 13:2: "Be not forgetful to entertain strangers: for thereby some have entertained angels unawares."

So don't be shocked if you experience something similar to what I have. In fact, I'm pretty sure you will, because God often sends us reminders and signs that we are on the right path. When you do receive a sign of Heavenly contact, please share it with me.

> "The door of the heavenly Kingdom is open to all, but the quality of men's merits will admit one man and reject another. How wretched must it be for a man to be shut from the glory of the saints and to be consigned with the devil to eternal flames."—Saint Bede the Venerable

Chapter Ten

Be the Woman God Wants You to Be

In a previous chapter, we saw what happens when weak-willed people turn their backs on God. Society collapses and billions of souls are condemned to the fires of hell.

It's not a coincidence that the infiltration and subversion of the Catholic Church took place at the same time that pornography became legal and spread its web over the land. Pornography weakens men and that is exactly what has been happening since the 1950s. Weak, feminized men were unable to resist the creation of the counterfeit church when it first appeared and they're unable to break away from it now.

At the same time that pornography became widespread, women's fashions changed. Skirts shortened, the bikini was introduced, and society was irreparably damaged. None of that happened by accident. It was all deliberately planned and carried out.

Changes in women's fashions are not your fault. The fault lies with generations of women before you who were conned into abandoning their roles as wives and mothers, and told to pursue "careers." Together with feminized men, they have systematically wrecked society and allowed the counterfeit church to come into existence and flourish.

While the failure is theirs, you have a duty to help clean up the mess they've made. To do that, you're going to have to think and act differently than almost every adult female you know.

Start that process by committing yourself to the four steps outlined in this book, and when it comes to abandoning sin, begin by changing the way you dress.

Dressing for the Devil

The sin of immodest dress is widespread and increasing by the day, with almost everyone in the world engaged in it on one level or another. In order to go to Heaven, you can't be like everyone else. You must dress modestly.

If you haven't figured it out yet, modern society is a funnel to hell. It's designed to suck as many souls down into hell as possible, and one of the ways it does that is by encouraging girls like you to dress immodestly.

Those who pull the strings of society are targeting you. They want you to dress immodestly in order to damn your soul to hell. Are you going to fall for their trap?

Girls see their peers immodestly dressed in movies, magazines, and television and receiving positive attention for it, so they imitate them. They think dressing immodestly is normal, because the media and all of society tell them it's normal. Even worse, the adult women in their life tell them it's normal and those women dress immodestly themselves. All of that leads girls your age and younger to dress immodestly and damn their souls to hell.

Anytime you see a girl showing her legs, her midriff, or any area of her body, you're looking at someone who's never had any guidance or honest advice in her life. You're looking at a girl with uncaring, brain-dead parents. You're looking at a girl under the influence of movies and television.

But it doesn't stop there. Movies and television teach girls that sexual appeal—not beauty, but sexual appeal—is all that matters. It encourages them to abandon their morals and religious beliefs and to engage in every form of sexual perversion imaginable, including adultery, homosexuality, trannyism, race-mixing, and more.

Society plays a part in this too. It encourages girls to hate men of their own race, while simultaneously engaging in as much sex as they can with men of other races. Then it encourages them to abort and murder their babies.

It's important for you to understand this and to know exactly what you're dealing with. You live in a world that attacks your purity in a thousand different ways through movies, music, television, magazines, advertising, and fashion. It's all in your face. Society wants to ensnare you in its satanic grasp and drag your soul to hell.

Don't let that happen.

One of the best things you could possibly do is to make a vow to God and to yourself that you will never dress immodestly again. And then keep that vow.

You won't attract as much attention from boys, but that's not a bad thing. By dressing modestly, you'll eliminate a lot of losers from your life. The boys you do attract will be of higher quality and treat you more respectfully. It's a win-win situation.

> "How many young girls there are who see nothing wrong in following certain shameless styles like so many sheep. They would certainly blush with shame if they could know the impression they make, and the feelings they evoke, in those who see them."—Pope Pius XII, 1954

In my neighborhood when the weather is warm, which is nine months out of the year, girls in their teens and twenties run around half-naked. I mean that literally. On any given day, you can spot dozens of them in a simple walk around the block. It's as commonplace as a person out walking their dog. And I'm sure my neighborhood is no different than thousands of other neighborhoods around the world.

Let's accompany one of those girls on her walk around the neighborhood and see just how damaging it is.

A Double-Edged Sword

Most sins hurt only one person—the person committing the sin. Immodest dress is different. It's one of the deadliest sins a person can engage in, because it casts a deep stain of sin on two parties—the person dressing immodestly and the person who witnesses it and thus engages in the sin of lust. That makes immodest dress a double-edged sword, and those who commit such a sin will be judged and damned twice, once for their own sin, and again for the sin of lust they encourage in others.

Imagine a girl dressed immodestly in tight clothing, in shorts, or in a short skirt, all of which society says are quite normal, on a simple trip to the corner store. Suppose on her trip that she draws the eyes of a hundred different people, either on foot or passing by in their cars, and suppose that half of those hundred people are men.

Out of those fifty men, forty-nine of them, upon seeing such a girl, are going to have an impure thought immediately flash across their mind.

That doesn't mean those forty-nine men are all sickos or perverts, although some of them probably are. The impure thought that flashes across their mind is merely a normal heterosexual reaction to the sight of a girl's bare legs or to a girl dressed in tight clothing.

Humans, like all animals, are designed to propagate the species. Thus, when a man sees a girl dressed immodestly, his normal biological reaction is to experience a lustful thought.

> "Above all, men are prone to the sin of impurity, to which nature itself inclines them."—Saint Alphonsus Liguori, *The Sermons of St. Alphonsus Liguori*

If it wasn't for male lust, the human race would have died out a long time ago. That's not to condone men for their sins. It's merely stating a fact.

Christian men at least make an attempt to control their biological urgings, but they are in the minority. Today the number of Christian men is very low and it's the primary reason for the downfall of society.

Take a look at 21st century Europe. Over the last twenty years, millions of rape-prone, non-Christian men have been purposely imported in order to destabilize the continent and eradicate Christianity. Sadly, they have succeeded.

Christianity in Europe today is practically non-existent; reduced to only a small remnant of faithful followers. Because Christianity has been all but eliminated, crime is everywhere. Churches are torched and burned. Murder and theft have reached unprecedented levels. Women and children by the thousands are beaten, gang-raped, and murdered. The entire continent has fallen.

Let's go back to our girl on the street. Out of those forty-nine men who experience an impure thought upon seeing her, a few will dismiss the thought the moment it reaches their mind, but the majority of men won't. They'll hold that impure thought in their head and expand on it.

Some of those forty-nine men will linger nearby and watch the girl. Others will follow her in order to get a closer look. Many of them will hold the image of the girl in their mind and masturbate to it when they get home. They'll picture the girl in their mind when they make love to their wife or girlfriend.

Others will be so triggered by the sight of the girl that they will resort to reading or watching pornography at the first chance they get.

Thus, in a single walk to the store, one girl, dressed the way society encourages her to dress, will share responsibility for the sins of dozens of men. *Men who had no intention of sinning before the girl crossed their path and drew their attention.*

A typical man might have been thinking about his job, or taking his kids to baseball practice, or a hundred other things when out of the blue a half-dressed girl suddenly appears before him and his attention is immediately diverted. Within seconds he is plunged into a vortex of sin.

Now multiply that one half-dressed girl by millions of other girls in neighborhoods all across the world and you have a level of sin that is simply mind-boggling to behold. Is it any wonder that souls fall like snowflakes into the never-ending fires of hell?

But surely, you say, it is unfair to blame the girl for the sins of the men.

Is it unfair? Yes, those forty-nine men should have had the presence of mind to banish the impure thought the moment it first occurred to them. But let us remember that men are weak and slaves to sin.

In today's world, men have no spiritual leadership or guidance. Because the Catholic Church has been infiltrated and a counterfeit church propped up in its place, men who remain outside of the traditional Catholic Church have nowhere to turn. They are set adrift on the sea of life with little to no religious instruction. They aren't taught how to avoid sin or that they should even try.

Yes, those forty-nine men are guilty of sin and they will be held accountable. However, they will be judged only for their own sins. The girl who inspired them to sin will be judged multiple times. She'll be judged not only for her own sin of dressing immodestly, but also for the untold number of sins she excited in others. What are the chances that such a person will be able to escape the torments of hell?

But wait—let's not forget that our imaginary sinner passed a hundred people on the street in her walk to the corner store, and that only half of the people she passed were men. The rest were women.

Of those fifty women, a good number of them will take note of the male attention the girl is attracting and decide to dress immodestly themselves at their next opportunity, in order to garner the same amount of attention for themselves.

Even worse, many of them will be young girls who up to this point have managed to cover themselves modestly. But now, upon seeing the attention our girl is receiving, they will be inspired to imitate her.

So now not only is our imaginary girl guilty of her own sin and the sins of the forty-nine men whose lustful thoughts she encouraged, she is also guilty of inspiring many of the women she passed on the street into dressing immodestly themselves. Many of them will be young girls, now corrupted for the remainder of their lives.

Imagine the immense scandal, the immense damning of souls caused by this one person, who through her own carelessness and vanity caused so many other people to sin along with her. She will be damning herself to hell for all eternity.

> "You carry your snare everywhere and spread your nets in all places. You allege that you never invited others to sin. You did not, indeed, by your words, but you have done so by your dress and your deportment and much more effectively than you could by your voice. When you have made another sin in his heart, how can you be innocent? Tell me, whom does this world condemn? Whom do judges in court punish? Those who drink the poison or those who prepare it and administer the fatal potion? You have prepared the abominable cup, you have given the death-dealing drink, and you are more criminal than those who poison the body; you murder not the body but the soul. And it is not to enemies you do this, nor are you urged on by any imaginary necessity, nor provoked by injury, but out of foolish vanity and pride."—Saint John Chrysostom

Multiply this one immodestly dressed girl by millions of other girls just like her and you can see the enormous amount of sin being committed on a daily basis by those who choose to dress immodestly.

You don't have to be one of them.

You can leave all the sinners behind and be one of the chosen few who ascends to Heaven. To do that, however, you must begin dressing modestly and never let up. Are you prepared to do that? Are you prepared to make a solemn promise to God to never dress immodestly again?

You're Not Alone

In her autobiography, Saint Teresa of Avila wrote: "If I were to offer some advice to parents, it would be this: pay attention to who it is that your children are associating with. Bad company can do a great deal of damage. This was certainly the case for me."

It was certainly the case for me too. Growing up, I let myself be led by others into so many dangerous, illegal, and sinful situations it was ridiculous. Granted, I went along with it. I was too stupid at the time to see what potential trouble I was headed for and I wanted to fit in with my "friends."

There were no adults in my life offering me any guidance at all. Not a single person with a brain in their head advising me on what to do or what not do. I certainly didn't have a book like this one to help me.

If you're in a similar situation, let me offer you some advice and hopeful words that were never offered by anyone to me. First of all, you're not alone. You have the entire history of Christian saints, including and especially the Blessed Virgin Mary and her spouse Joseph to help you.

God sent us these saints as guides. They're available for us to call on 24/7. All you have to do is ask them for help. Many of them, such as Saint Agnes and Saint Maria Goretti, died upholding their purity. You can ask them for help.

Saint Agnes was only thirteen when she refused marriage to a non-Christian man who reported her to the governor. The governor sentenced Agnes to be taken to a brothel and raped. She was dragged naked through the streets to the brothel, but every man who tried to rape her there was struck blind. The governor was so enraged he had her beheaded.

That's the price many saints paid in order to uphold their purity. They would be shocked speechless if they saw the way so many women and young girls dressed today and how little purity is respected.

In addition to asking the saints for help, you can surround yourself with holy books and refer to them for inspiration.

You can seek like-minded companions, people who value salvation as highly as you do, although finding them won't be easy. Let them know upfront that going to Heaven is your first priority. Of course, I will always be in your corner.

Make a Vow of Modesty

The bottom line is that any article of clothing that is too revealing or too form-fitting is a sin for you to wear. So get rid of it. Toss it overboard.

Now, what if it's difficult for you to find modest clothes to wear? What if all you can find are clothes either too revealing or too tight-fitting?

I would call that a tremendous business opportunity.

If no one is offering tasteful, yet modest clothing for sale, you can be the first. If others are already doing it, but their clothes are unappealing or priced too high, you can be the first there too, by producing modest clothing that is both appealing and reasonably priced.

What's more, if you design and wear your own clothes, you'll be a walking billboard for your business. Others will stop and ask you where you bought what you're wearing and you'll have instant customers wherever you go.

Not only will you be dressing modestly yourself and providing for both you and your family in an honest and life-affirming way, you'll also be helping other young women to dress modestly, which will earn you great merits in Heaven.

NOTE: If you're a guy reading this, everything here applies to you too. From this day forward, you must never allow yourself to dress immodestly or be seen in any state of undress. That means you must never again attend a public pool or beach or be seen shirtless in any way.

You Will Encounter Resistance

As you make the necessary changes in your life that you must make in order to go to Heaven, you will meet with resistance. However, you should know that the only people who are going to object to your dressing modestly are those leading sinful lives.

They want you to continue dressing immodestly and committing sin, because if you don't, it forces them to confront their own sinful life. There's nothing a sinner hates more than being reminded that they're on the road to hell. Anyone who takes issue with your decision to dress modestly should be purged from your life. You're better off without them.

Only the strongest of the strong make it to Heaven. As you move ever closer to that goal, your eyes will be opened in the most incredible ways. You'll see sinners all around you, including among your closest friends and relatives. You won't see politicians, entertainers, or celebrities anymore. You'll see liars, thieves, and cheats. You'll see child molesters, tyrants, narcissists, fools, and puppets engaged in the most horrible sins imaginable. Thank God you're not one of them.

Lead a No-Fault Life

We spoke earlier about the many miracles attributed to the Catholic Church. One miracle we didn't mention—and like the others, it's *only* found in the Catholic Church, not in any other religion—are the thousands of documented cases in which God has allowed someone who has died to reveal their status in the afterlife to someone still living.

Almost all of these cases involve a person in purgatory asking one of the living to pray for their delivery to Heaven.

> 2 Machabees 12:46: "It is therefore a holy and wholesome thought to pray for the dead, that they may be loosed from sins."

If you don't know about purgatory, it's where the souls of baptized Catholics go when they die in a state of grace, but are not yet pure enough to enter Heaven. (When a non-Catholic person dies, including anyone who adheres to the counterfeit church, they go straight to hell.)

Souls in purgatory experience similar sufferings as those in hell. When one of these souls makes their presence known to a person still living, they often appear in the midst of fire and suffering the worst torments. Just like in hell, the fire of purgatory burns with the most violent pain, but it doesn't kill the soul and it never ends. You can imagine the misery these poor souls endure. In every case in which one of these suffering souls has appeared to the living, they've said that no pain on earth comes close to the pain experienced in purgatory.

Saint Cyril confirmed this when he said, "It would be better to suffer all the possible torments of earth until Judgment Day than to pass one day in Purgatory."

> Matthew 5:25: "Verily, I say unto thee, Thou shalt by no means come out thence, till thou hast paid the uttermost farthing."

Now there are two very important points I want you to take away from this. The first is the immense obligation we have to pray for the souls in purgatory. They cannot help themselves. All they can do is suffer—and suffer harshly. We have a sacred duty to pray for them, to ease their suffering and to help send them to Heaven.

The second thing I want you take away from this is that in each and every case where a soul in purgatory has appeared to a person here on earth, they have stressed that the souls in purgatory are being punished for the slightest of faults; for transgressions that we consider almost inconsequential here on earth. And not only are they punished for these minor faults, they are punished for years, decades even, or in some cases centuries.

Saint Peter Damian was visited by his deceased sister, who revealed to him that she was sentenced to many years in purgatory for listening to an "evil song." (One can only imagine how tame the song she listened to was compared to the music being pumped out today on the radio, on websites and in concerts.)

Saint Vincent Ferrer was also visited by his deceased sister. She appeared to him surrounded by flames and suffering the worst torments. She told her brother she would be in Purgatory until the end of time as punishment for enjoying worldly pleasures and she begged him for his assistance.

At the apparitions of Fatima, one of the first questions the young seers asked of their visitor from Heaven was the status of two young girls who had recently died:

> "Is Maria da Neves now in Heaven?"
> "Yes, she is."
> "And Amelia?"
> "She will be in purgatory until the end of the world."
> Purgatory! The end of the world!
> —William Thomas Walsh, *Our Lady of Fatima*

Amelia was a poor peasant girl. She didn't murder anyone. She didn't commit the sin of abortion. She wasn't a thief. She almost certainly died a virgin. What could she have possibly done to merit suffering in the flames of Purgatory *until the end of the world*? Perhaps she dressed immodestly and inspired others to sin.

When Saint Magdalene de Pazzi was shown a vision of Purgatory, she cried out in horror, "Good God! How they are tormented!" She saw souls being punished for years for such trivial sins as ambition, pride, impatience, ingratitude, hypocrisy, and weakness.

Sister Francesca of Pampelona was visited by hundreds of souls suffering in purgatory. It was made known to her that most souls remain in purgatory an average of fifty years. She saw a man who suffered fifty-nine years in purgatory for worldliness—that is, for always trying to make his life as easy and as comfortable as possible; and another man in purgatory sixty-four years for playing cards for money.

She saw many nuns of her Carmelite order suffering in purgatory for decades, including nuns who had worked miracles in their own life. (*Purgatory* by Father Frederick William Faber)

If miracle-working nuns can suffer for decades in purgatory before being purified enough to enter Heaven, what's to become of us?

In answer to that question, I urge you to lead as faultless a life as possible; to go out of your way to avoid any sinful or questionable behavior, no matter how trivial.

Matthew 12:36: "But I say unto you, That every idle word that men shall speak, they shall give account thereof in the day of judgment."

The best way to do that is to avoid other people, as we covered earlier. However, there are two additional things you can do in order to lead a faultless life and increase your chances of going straight to Heaven. The first is to avoid social media.

Social media is the biggest time waster in the world. Even worse, it encourages all manner of sinful behavior from its participants, almost all of whom are people of bad will.

By engaging others on social media, you are throwing yourself into a mix of sinners and mentally deranged deviants. Like a rat scavenging for food, you'll find yourself clicking back to your previous posts, searching for the number of "likes" or "dislikes." Your "likes" will inflate your ego and serve the same purpose as finding a morsel of food does to a starving rat. However, just like that morsel of food, your social media "likes" will only sustain you for so long, until hunger in the way of approval from others gnaws again at your stomach.

Meanwhile, every "dislike" or negative comment you receive will stir you to anger and make you respond in kind by lashing out via your keyboard at total strangers. Before you know it, you will be that starving rat, forever seeking, but never finding.

That's what social media does to people.

You might be interested to know that all of the so-called "influencers" you encounter on social media are nothing but frauds and traitors. Many of them were paid hundreds of thousands of dollars to shill the Stupid-19 vaccine, which they did—promoting the deadly jab to all of their followers. They lied through their teeth for money and attention.

Today dozens of those same "influencers" who took the jab are dead or in the process of dying from cancer. They had no qualms about promoting a deadly bioweapon to their followers in exchange for money and now they're either in hell or on their way to hell for doing so. You can't say they don't deserve it. Stay away from social media.

Homeschooling is Best

Another thing you can do to help lead a faultless life and increase your chances of going straight to Heaven is to begin homeschooling. In fact, your life would be a hundred times better if you immediately stopped attending school and began homeschooling. The main reason for that is because your teachers are all lying to you.

Are they claiming that "Joe Biden" won the 2020 presidential election?

Are they alleging that all religions are equal and worthy of the same respect?

Are they insisting that men can be women or that women can be men?

Are they insinuating that the phony pandemic of 2020-2023 was a real thing?

Are they inferring that truth is relative and a matter of opinion?

Are they telling you that the attacks of 9/11 were orchestrated by Osama bin Laden and carried out by nineteen guys with box cutters?

Well, guess what? They're lying to you.

Even worse, your brain-dead classmates are buying those lies. Some of your classmates, anyway. There might be a few mentally sharp students at your school who know what's going on in the world. But knowing people the way I do, I doubt it.

If your teachers are pushing any of the lies outlined above, and I'll bet that they are, then you would benefit tremendously by choosing to homeschool.

Lies are like cockroaches, there's never just one. If your teachers are lying to you about the stolen election, false religions, gender confusion, the phony pandemic, or the attacks of 9/11, then they are lying to you about everything else. And if that's the case, what kind of an education are you getting? It sounds to me like you're being indoctrinated, not educated.

Not only are you being lied to at school, you have sick and twisted teachers trying to groom and indoctrinate you and your classmates into homosexuality, trannyism, and other sick perversions. They're not just doing that to people your own age either. They're doing it to children as young as three, four, and five. They're *salivating* at the chance to molest and sexually mutilate those precious young children. These are sick, sick people we're talking about. For the sake of your soul, purge them all from your life and do it immediately.

In fact, on that issue alone you should tell your school to shove it and start homeschooling. Ask your parents about it. Ask them how they can justify spending money to send you to a school that employs teachers who want to groom, molest, and sexually mutilate innocent little children. Let me know what they say.

There are no advantages to your remaining in school. Seriously, can you name one? Unless you enjoy listening to teachers who aren't qualified to clean a horse stall tell one lie after another, what possible benefit are you deriving from continuing to attend school?

When you attend school you also put yourself in daily contact with hundreds of people your own age, any one of whom could have a disastrous effect on your life by leading you to sin.

We discussed that in depth earlier in this book, but it needs to be repeated. The most common cause of sin is other people. Being around them creates a constant source of temptation. I know very few people who are able to resist it.

Not only that, but many of your classmates are brainwashed to the point where they actually support the sick and perverted teachers who want to molest and sexually mutilate children. You don't want to be around anyone like that, not for one second.

Being around such people, going to parties, going to dances . . . you're going to be subjected to one temptation after another.

You'll be pushed to drink alcohol and take drugs. Neither of which you should engage in. Drinking one beer or taking one hit on a joint isn't going to kill you. But it will make you prone to drinking a second beer or taking a second hit on a joint, followed by a third, and a fourth. Soon you'll be hooked. Like masturbation, if you do it once, you're likely to do it again . . . and again.

Beer is literally liquid estrogen, which is a female sex hormone. It's one of the worst things you can put into your body, and taking drugs will kill you.

I can't tell you how many people I know who fried their brains from drugs and alcohol. Most are dead, but a few are still living. They're shells of their former selves; barely able to function. The best way to avoid such a fate yourself is to never start drinking and to never take any drugs at all.

Wherever alcohol is available you have people who drink to excess, and when people drink to excess they lose their ability to think clearly. When you realize how most people are incapable of thinking clearly when they're sober, you can imagine how stupid they become when they're drunk.

If you're at a party, nightclub, or bar where alcohol is served, you'll find yourself surrounded by drunken louts. Sooner or later a fight will break out and then all of those drunken fools will take to the road, putting themselves and others at risk of a tragic accident. The best way to handle that situation is to not go to such places to begin with.

As for drugs, did you know that the Bible teaches that all drugs are sorcery and witchcraft? It's true. There's a book called *Strong's Concordance*, which contains the Hebrew and Greek translations for every word in both the Old and New Testament in the Bible. If you take that book, and put it next to your King James Bible, and then open your Bible to Revelations 18:23, and look at the last sentence, it reads, "For thy merchants were the great men of the earth, for by thy sorceries were all nations deceived."

Then open your *Strong's Concordance* to the Main Concordance and look up the word "sorceries." Scroll down the list under that word to Revelations 18:23 or Re 18:23. Next to that it will say, "by thy s were all nations deceived," followed by the number 5331.

Turn to the back of the book where the Greek translations are, locate that same number, and you'll see that it says, "pharmakeia from 5332; medication ('pharmacy'), i.e. magic, sorcery, witchcraft." If you scroll down, you'll see that it also says, "Pharmakon; a druggist or poisoner, i.e. a magician, sorcerer."

The Bible has always taught that drugs are sorcery and that those who dispense them are sorcerers, witches and poisoners. Weak-willed women and feminized men don't want to admit that because they're cowards and prefer to hide from the truth, but there it is. Now you know the truth.

Everyone You Meet Today is Mentally Deranged

From the time the fake pandemic began in February of 2020 until the end of 2022, I was the only person—and I mean the *only* person—within a five mile radius of my neighborhood not wearing a mask. At first, the streets were deserted and I enjoyed walking the sidewalks alone. But then they appeared . . . zombies in face masks . . . thousands of them.

It got to the point where I had to put a note on the inside of my front door, something I would see every day just before leaving the house. The note said, "Everyone you meet today is mentally deranged." I needed that note as a constant reminder that I was about to step into a world of madness.

As you learn more about life, you'll start to feel the same way. You are going to find yourself to be the lone voice of reason in a sea of idiotic dissent. It's going to appear to you that everyone you meet is mentally deranged and they will be, including your classmates. They will be operating on false beliefs fueled by the mainstream media and reinforced by your teachers and school administrators. You will be the only one who is actually living in reality.

That's why homeschooling is so important to you at this stage of your life. I suggest you get some information on the subject of homeschooling as soon as possible, study the contents, and then present it to your parents.

If you have younger brothers or sisters attending school, then you're going to have to push your parents—and I mean push them hard—to get your younger siblings out of school and into homeschooling. If they're attending school now, then it's obvious that no one is looking out for them.

That means you're going to have to do it.

Whether your parents allow you to homeschool or not, one thing you should do as soon as possible is sit down with a school counselor (pick the one who is less of an idiot than all of the others) and find out what you need to do in order to graduate in three years instead of four.

Yes, it's possible to do that, to graduate in three years. Find out what the requirements are and then adjust your life so you are able to complete them. That will shave one year off your time spent in the insane asylum.

You can also graduate from college in three years and if you intend on going to college, you should find out what those requirements are too so you can fulfill them. Why waste four years in either high school or college when you can graduate in three? In fact, if you're in a big hurry, you can take a GED (General Education Development) test at any age and not even bother with high school.

If you've read this far into this book, then you obviously possess a superior intellect. You could probably take the GED test and pass it right now. You can even take practice tests just to make sure. If you pass the GED, you can then go straight to college, or better yet, straight to pursuing your life's work—which is making sure you go to Heaven.

Never forget that going to Heaven *is* your life's work. It's not your "career" or anything else. In fact, anyone who tells you to "follow your dreams," "pursue your passion," or "focus on your career," is an idiot who should never be listened to again. Your passion, your dream, and your "career" are going to Heaven, period.

I wish I had taken the GED test when I was sixteen. Only nobody told me about it. If I had known, I would have taken and passed the test right then and there. But I didn't know that such a thing as a GED test even existed. I had no guidance. I had no one offering me any good advice. I certainly didn't have a book like this one. But you do. And now you know about getting a GED. Give it some serious thought.

Don't be put off that it's not an actual diploma. In life, nobody cares about such things. No one will ever ask to see your high school diploma or your grades.

I've produced and starred in movies, won screenwriting contests, written over twenty books, ran a business, supervised hundreds of employees, been interviewed countless times on television and radio, given numerous public talks and no one has ever asked to see my high school diploma or my grades. If I had brought the subject up, they would have laughed me out of the room.

Unless you're aiming for an academic scholarship, what you achieve in high school means absolutely nothing in the real world. So why not get a GED or graduate in three years and kiss the dump goodbye?

About College

Is college right for you?

I know every adult in your life has told you it is, but is it really? If you think the amount of lies you're being told in high school is bad, just wait until you go to college. You'll be hit with a virtual tidal wave of lies and surrounded by so many brainless idiots you'll feel like you've stumbled into a mental ward.

Colleges today are indoctrination centers where independent thinking is stamped out and minds are molded into liberal mush. Spending four years in college is equivalent to getting a lobotomy.

The level of disinformation and stupidity running rampant on college campuses is so high it is simply mind-boggling to comprehend. And for what?

Today a college degree is essentially worthless. Over half of the employers in the country now hold it against an applicant if they have a college degree. They know that anyone who has spent four years in college has been dumbed down to a point that is irreparable.

Consider college carefully. Aside from the study of law and engineering, there's nothing you can learn in college that you can't learn better on your own. That goes for high school too. There's nothing being taught in that zoo you call high school that you can't learn better on your own.

Remember, whatever you achieve in this life in regards to education, a so-called career, or worldly success means nothing when it comes to going to Heaven.

Also, remember that the education system in this country for the last fifty or more years has served as a foil to Christ; a counter to Christ. And because Christ is God, and God is truth, then because the education system runs counter to Christ, it also runs counter to truth.

As it currently stands, the education system in America exists to lead people away from God. Nowhere is that more true than in college. If you attend college, you will be fed a non-stop diet of lies and led far away from God.

Should You Have Children?

Women are meant to be mothers. That is their highest calling. I know it doesn't seem that way, because everything and everyone in modern society is telling you the opposite. But bear in mind, they're all going to hell. To avoid that same fate for yourself, you have to think and act the exact opposite of how everyone else is thinking and acting.

The problem with being a parent is that the moment your first child is born, you are entering a lifelong fight. You'll be fighting with idiot, quack doctors who want to pump your child full of drugs and "vaccines" that cause autism, paralysis, and death.

You'll be fighting with pink-haired Communist teachers who want to sexually mutilate your children and groom them into homosexuality and other sick perversions.

You'll be fighting with the idiot parents of other children who can't comprehend why you won't "get with the program" and pump your kids full of drugs and deadly "vaccines;" why you won't allow your children to be sexually mutilated and molested; why you won't let your child play with their "Johnny," who thinks he's a girl and wears a red dress.

And that's just the tip of the iceberg.

So you've got some tough decisions to make. Having sex outside of marriage is a mortal sin, so you can't do that. Birth control and family planning are also mortal sins, so if you do get married you'll have to have children and lots of them. And from that point on, your life will be one big headache.

Finally, keep in mind that parents are responsible for the spiritual wellbeing of their children. In other words, if your children don't make it to Heaven, you will be held responsible. That almost necessitates that you have a strong command of Catholic doctrine before you even think about having children.

What's my advice?

It's going to be the toughest thing you ever did in your life, but I advise you to remain single and celibate and focus on going to Heaven.

Words of Hope, Meant Just for You

As you can gather by now, going to Heaven is a process of letting go. Letting go of sinful behavior; letting go of sinful people, places, and pastimes; letting go of all the so-called pleasure of this world, no matter how enticing; letting go of false religions, false ideologies, and false beliefs. Only after one has let go of all of those things, is enough space cleared out for God to come in.

Don't be a wimp about this. Don't be afraid to cut people, places, and things out of your life. The world is already filled with wimps. God doesn't need wimps. He needs warriors.

If you become a warrior for God, and I encourage you to do so, you will be a rare and courageous individual. And because warriors for God are so rare, you will likely have to travel your road alone. There's nothing wrong with that. Almost everyone that we know with a high degree of certainty is now in Heaven made their journey alone.

The herd will not be there with you on Judgment Day. It will be you alone with God. All of those weak-willed wimps who turned their backs on God in this life will be cast into the lake of fire in the next. Meanwhile, those who dedicate their lives to God and embrace the Catholic Faith without compromise will enjoy everlasting life in paradise.

You can count on me being in your corner. And you can count on Jesus standing solidly alongside of you. He was on His own too. When Jesus was arrested, all of the Apostles except Peter fled for their lives. But then Peter denied Jesus three times and Christ went to his crucifixion alone.

You may have to do the same. From this point forward you are your own best friend. Actually, I take that back. God is your best friend. And who could ask for a better best friend than God? God is fiercely loyal. If you show up for Him, He'll show up for you.

"The world is rotten because of silence."—Saint Catherine of Sienna

Chapter Eleven

Heaven—You're Almost There!

Congratulations! You now have all the information you need to secure your salvation in Heaven. All that's left for you to do is to apply what you've learned in this book.

Think about it. If you're a member of the true Church of Jesus Christ—the traditional Catholic Church—and you are committed to withdrawing from the world, practicing daily prayer, and leading a sinless life, which includes periodic confession to a validly ordained priest, then it is virtually impossible for you *not* to go to Heaven. All that's required on your part is persistence.

There are additional things you can do to earn merits in Heaven and I recommend doing them.

You can evangelize others and help convert them to the true Faith. (That's my motivation in writing this book.) Only don't be surprised or discouraged if your efforts fail. Some people are so filled with bad will and so obstinate in their false beliefs that they will never be converted.

That's on them, not you.

You can practice acts of mortification.

You can read holy books—I have a list of recommended books for free if you email me.

You can make sacrifices for sinners (this is one of the messages from Fatima).

You can pray and make sacrifices for the souls in Purgatory. Praying for the souls in Purgatory is huge and will help you tremendously in your quest to go to Heaven.

> Machabees 12:46: "It is therefore a holy and wholesome thought to pray for the dead, that they may be loosed from sins."

You can donate money or time to worthwhile Catholic organizations. The catch there is that at the time of this writing there is only one such organization in the entire world—only one place on earth that is spreading true Catholic doctrine and helping to save souls. You can find them at www.MostHolyFamilyMonastery.com Donating time or money to other organizations is actually a sin as they are not spreading true Catholic doctrine.

All of these acts will help you in your journey to Heaven. But the big four are avoiding sin, practicing daily prayer, withdrawing from the world, and embracing the traditional Catholic Faith. With those in your pocket you are guaranteed to succeed. You may have to spend some time in Purgatory in expiation for past sins, but you know for a fact that you won't be going to hell, like the vast majority of the human race.

And eventually your time in Purgatory will be up and you'll proceed on to Heaven.

You will then be a member of that small, select club; the fewest of the few, the strongest of the strong. Give yourself a pat on the back. You're almost there.

Easy to Say No

The path to Heaven that lies ahead of you is so simple that you may wonder why everyone isn't doing it. The reason why others are not doing it, if you haven't already guessed, is bad will. And, as we discussed earlier, bad will stems from pride.

People would rather remain haughty and proud—*even if it means going to hell*—than humble themselves and go to Heaven. They are living in a state that can only be described as arrogant blindness.

You're going to be stunned as you begin to observe this in your own life. It won't be only obvious sinners and heretics that you see rejecting Heaven, but also plenty of "nice people." In fact, nice people are often the most prideful and sinful of all.

The sheer number of people in your life who choose to remain blind and condemn themselves to hell will be so great you'll wonder whether the entire world is under some sort of satanic spell. (It is.)

And it all goes back to people not wanting restrictions on their sins. In essence, that is what it all boils down to. That's the whole of it. People just don't want to give up their sins.

Even worse, they refuse to give up those sinful passions despite knowing full well that those very same passions are leading them straight to hell.

Actually, not all of them know they're on the road to hell. There are millions of people who are so far removed from reality they have no idea who they are, where they're going, or what they're doing. You could call them mentally ill and you would be right, but it's actually much deeper than that.

Saint Bruno said, "He hath a demon within him who persists in any grave sin." I think he hit the nail on the head. People are demonically possessed and in a state of permanent brain fog and they don't even know it. Until the demon possessing them is cast out through daily recitation of the Rosary, there's really no hope for them.

I've seen people break free from their Fake News programming through intelligent and applied research, but I've never seen anyone break free from demonic possession without daily recitation of the Rosary and conversion to the Catholic Faith. It just can't be done any other way.

It's a sad situation, because refusal to save one's own soul is a form of suicide—suicide of the soul. And just as those who commit physical suicide cause immense harm and grief to those around them, so do those who commit suicide of the soul. By selfishly refusing to save themselves from hell, they crush the hearts of everyone around them.

Such behavior earns them eternal membership in the Stupid Club, the most popular club on earth.

Thank God you're not one of them. In fact, from this day forward, you'll be the smartest person in every room you're in, because you'll be the only one pursuing a path to Heaven. Everyone else will be focused on earthly "success" and the things of this world. You'll have your eyes on the bigger picture and an infinitely greater prize.

Total Redemption

Now I want to share a secret with you. A great secret that very few people know about. It comes in two parts.

I could have shared this secret much earlier, but I didn't, because I wanted to save it only for those who are serious about going to Heaven. This late in the book, the dabblers have drifted away and the people of bad will are long gone. If you've read this far, you're one of the serious ones.

The first part of this secret concerns you. If you manage to make it to Heaven, and you will if you refrain from sin, pray every day, withdraw from the world, and hold the Catholic Faith without compromise, then you will have achieved something so stupendous it's simply beyond words.

According to Saint Vincent Ferrer, from the story related by Saint Leonard of Port Maurice (page 17), out of every 33,000 people who die, only two of them go straight to Heaven and three go to Purgatory. The rest all go to hell. That makes the percentage of people who eventually end up in Heaven .00015.

Now if we consider that both Saint Bernard and the archdeacon of Lyons in Saint Vincent's story were extremely holy men and that almost no one today is at their level of spirituality, then the percentage of people going to Heaven is much smaller than .00015. In fact, it's so small as to be almost infinitesimal. Yet you will have done it.

What that means for you is total redemption.

By going to Heaven, you can right every wrong from your past. You can erase every mistake you've ever made. You can wipe clean your entire slate.

Think about that. Everything you've ever done that hurt another person or caused them despair will be forgiven. Every fault you've ever had will be corrected.

Have you ever hurt someone to the point where it pains you just to think about it?

That pain will be washed away.

Have you ever sinned to the point where it looks as if all hope is gone?

That hopelessness will be replaced by joy.

I don't care if you're sitting on death row, guilty of taking another man's life. I don't care if you murdered your own child through an abortion, the most horrible sin imaginable. I don't care if you've spent your entire life hurting other people and running roughshod over them. You can be forgiven of all those sins and enjoy everlasting paradise in Heaven, where you'll be loved by God and all of His angels.

It's the same with all the disappointments that life has thrown your way. All of the things you've dreamed of having but never did will mean nothing.

If you've ever suffered a broken heart, your heart will be healed.

If you've ever looked with longing upon the things of this world, your longing will cease.

If you've ever felt sad and lonely because you never achieved the fame or fortune you so desperately craved, none of that will matter anymore. It will all be washed clean, because you will have achieved the ultimate victory.

If you've spent your life wishing you were prettier, handsomer, more attractive, know that in God's eyes—and God's eyes are the only ones that count—you are beautiful beyond measure. In Heaven you will radiate with a beauty that the human mind cannot even begin to comprehend.

If life has thrown you curve balls; if you've suffered one setback after another; if you have experienced trials and tribulations that left you broken and in tears, then know this: Your glory in Heaven will be greater than any earthly success you could possibly imagine.

If you make it to Heaven—and you will, I promise you, as long as you follow in the footsteps of those who are already there—then everything in your past will have been perfect, because it will have led you to life's greatest prize.

Through penance and humility and the sacrament of confession you can not only redeem yourself and undo the damage of your past sins, you can rise to greater spiritual heights than those from which you fell.

Saint Damian says you can redeem yourself to such an extent as to restore the moral state of virginity.

That's the first part of the secret. The second part concerns other people. Not only will going to Heaven allow you to redeem your entire life, but you can do the same for others. You can help them redeem their past and achieve eternal salvation. By offering up your prayers and sacrifices to God on behalf of others, you can convert them to the Catholic Faith, you can remove their addiction to sin, and you can literally save their souls.

Are there people you love? People who were kind to you and helped you along the way? People you always liked, but lost contact with? People you would love to see again?

Here's your chance to do just that. To not only see those people again, but to help them in the most glorious way possible by helping them go to Heaven through your prayers, sacrifices, and sufferings.

The Church is replete with thousands of examples of faithful souls doing just that—offering prayers and sacrifices in order to save the souls of those they loved—and succeeding.

Here's the thing though, in order to help others go to Heaven, you must remain free from sin and hold the Catholic Faith without compromise or your prayers won't be heard.

> "Now we know that God heareth no sinners: but if any man be a worshipper of God, and doeth his will, him he heareth."—John 9:31

> "He that turneth away his ears from hearing the law, his prayer shall be an abomination."—Proverbs 28:9

> "We know that God does not hear sinners."—Saint Robert Bellarmine

Can you imagine anything greater than helping those you love achieve eternal salvation in Heaven? I can't.

The door is open. God is waiting for you to surrender to Him and take that step. Are you ready?

Your Dream Date with Heaven

Remember your first date? Remember the effort you put in beforehand. Remember how you cleaned your house, washed your car, and made yourself presentable?

If you had a future date scheduled with someone of great importance to you, would you not prepare yourself to the utmost in terms of grooming and dress? Would you not see that your home was sparkling with cleanliness in order to make a good impression? Would you not take great pains with your appearance in order to look as good as you possibly can?

Certainly you would. And if that is the case, why not begin to prepare yourself now for the ultimate date that awaits you—your date with Heaven.

Don't look at death with a sense of morbidity, but a sense of wonder and joy. You will see the face of Jesus; perhaps even of Mary, your mother. How can that be morbid?

You will see your guardian angel for the first time, the angel who stuck with you every step of the way, from the hour of your birth to the hour of your death.

You might see choirs of angels. You might see people you love, long passed and now waiting for you with open arms. It will be the most important date of your life, your dream date with Heaven. Why not begin preparing for it now? Why not cleanse your soul and beautify yourself so you are ready?

Prepare for that moment by purging from your life everything and anything that could possibly tempt you to sin. Make time every day to pray. Withdraw from the world. Firmly resolve to hold the fullness of the Catholic Faith without compromise.

Your dream date with Heaven is approaching.

Every tick of the clock brings it closer.

Words of Hope, Meant Just for You

We've come a long way, you and I, through the pages of this book. And we're each a different person now than we were when we began. Both of us are now closer to God, closer to Heaven. The only thing left to do is to put into practice what we've learned.

I hate to say goodbye, so I won't.

Instead I'll say, "See you in Heaven!"

I can't wait to meet you there!

"One is where he is before God and nothing more, even if he himself and everyone else thinks otherwise."—Saint Basil

Thank You!

Thank you very much for reading this book. If you enjoyed it, please leave a review so that others will be inspired to read it too. *Your review of this book could actually save someone's soul.* Imagine that.

If you would like clarification about anything you read here, or if I can help you in any way, please contact me.

If you would like to join my Intelligence Report email list and receive expert analysis of world events, email me for details.

You can email me here:

mainsmike@yahoo.com

I truly hope you adopt the advice in this book. As I said from the outset: I want to see you in Heaven.

Other books by Mike Mains

The Impostor Sister Lucy

Lucy Santos was one of the three seers of Fatima, where the Miracle of the Sun took place in 1917, and where she was entrusted with the legendary Third Secret of Fatima—a secret so profound it's rumored to have apocalyptic significance.

Lucy later became a nun, but then something strange happened to her around the year 1960. Her appearance changed radically. Most shockingly, she began committing public acts of heresy that were unthinkable and in conflict with her character. Why did that happen? In this explosive new book, you will discover:

- Conclusive proof that Sister Lucy was indeed replaced with an impostor.
- Why the Vatican had to replace Sister Lucy with an impostor.
- Sister Lucy's frank admission that we are living in the end times.
- The true story of the Consecration of Russia—was it really done?
- The explosive contents of the Third Secret, never before revealed.

This is a must-read book for Catholics and for anyone who has ever studied or wondered about the events of Fatima. Pour yourself a cup of hot chocolate and curl up on the couch. You're about to read one the most amazing stories in the history of the world.

The Imposter Sister Lucy: https://amzn.to/2QXq57o

"**Very well-written**, and it is **indisputable that the pictures portray two different women.**"

"**Nourishes the Mind and Soul.**"

"Fatima is real, but **the Sister Lucy presented by the Church after 1957 is not the same woman.**"

"**The author presents all the evidence** and persuasively argues **that Sister Lucy was replaced by a double** in about 1960."

"**Real fascinating book—an eye-opener for sure!**"

"**Every Catholic Needs to Read This Book!**"

"This was **a great read** that everyone in the true church needs to read. **It contains facts and truths.**"

How to Go to Heaven for Teen Boys
How to Go to Heaven for Teen Girls

The books *How to Go to Heaven for Teen Boys* and *How to Go to Heaven for Teen Girls* contain the complete text to *How to Go to Heaven*, but with additional chapters on the temptations that young people face, such as drug and alcohol use, pornography, immodest dress, the loss of purity, etc.

God and Your Health

Are you dealing with challenging health issues? Has your doctor told you that your condition is "incurable"? Don't believe it for a second. God in His infinite mercy has provided us with the remedies we need to heal any disease. However, God sometimes sends us an illness as a wakeup call, to get our attention and bring us closer to Him.

If you want to know more about the connection between God and your health, then this is the book for you. Inside you will find information on how to heal any disease under the sun, as well as startling revelations on the relationship between God and a healthy life.

Available in summer 2024.

God and Money

How does God feel about money? Does He want you to be rich? Does He want you to be poor? Read this fascinating new book and discover for yourself:

- How God views money.
- Why Jesus spoke about money so often in His parables.
- Why the Bible says the love of money and not money itself is the root of all evil.
- The exact amount of money God wants you to have.
- The three principles of money.
- Why men pursue money, and why women pursue men who have money.

And so much more. Available in summer 2024.

Bodybuilding for Boys & Young Men

If you want muscles and you want them fast, this is the book for you. It's all here: what exercises to do, how often to do them, what to eat, even how to think. A fast, fun, and effective way to build your body with a 100% success rate.

The North Hollywood Detective Club Series

This mystery book series came about because I couldn't find any books for young readers aged 10-15 that weren't pumped full of anti-Christian, anti-family messaging.

Believe me, I tried. I searched the entirety of Amazon, as well as my local library, only to find that literally every book published for young readers over the last forty-plus years contained some sort of Godless content.

Either the stories centered on witches, werewolves, or demons; or they featured sometimes subtle, sometimes not-so-subtle, anti-Christian content. Every single one.

On top of all that, the writing wasn't so good. It was passable, but almost never beyond that.

Unable to find any appropriate books for young readers that I could recommend to others or give away as gifts, I created my own. The response has been tremendous. If you're looking for clean and exciting mystery and suspense books for young readers, you've just struck gold.

The Case of the Hollywood Art Heist

Jeffrey Jones is a kid with a problem. A *lot* of problems. He's laughed at in school. The neighborhood bully has it out for him. And his parents treat him like a six-year-old. However, Jeffrey does have one ace up his sleeve: He's a master investigator, able to piece together clues and solve impossible crimes.

When the brother of a classmate is arrested for stealing a valuable painting, Jeffrey and his best friend Pablo jump into action and form The North Hollywood Detective Club to investigate the crime. Can two teenage detectives save the day and rescue an innocent man from jail?

"**Utterly fantastic!!!!!** I absolutely adored this novel. **As a 13 year old girl I have found friendship, mystery and enjoyment of this book.** It was such a great book that I stayed up until 1:32 am!!!!"

"**Magnificent Mystery!** I am always looking for that book that will hold me on the edge of my seat all the way through. This author has done that. I have just a handful of mystery authors that I recommend on a regular basis to my students. I now have a new one to recommend when the school year begins."

"Just a short note to let you know that **I have assigned your book, 'The North Hollywood Detective Club' as one of the textbooks at our little school,** which is located right outside Paris, France."

The Case of the Dead Man's Treasure

When Jeffrey's high school teacher hires him to find the driver responsible for a hit-and-run car accident, he thinks it's an easy case—until it leads to a harrowing encounter with a ruthless criminal and the clues to a hidden treasure. Now he and his friends are in a race against time with a trio of sinister treasure hunters who will stop at nothing to get their hands on the prize. Who will find the treasure first?

"My 12-year-old loved this book. I read it to him at night before bed. Highly recommend it."

"My 13 year-old daughter loves this series."

"Really good book. I recommend it to people who love Sherlock Holmes and detective/mystery books because it is **well plotted out.** Mains did a great job."

The Case of the Christmas Counterfeiters

While the rest of the world prepares to celebrate Christmas, 15-year-old Jeffrey and his friends stumble upon a plot to flood Los Angeles with billions of dollars in counterfeit currency. Their investigation leads them to a master criminal, his hoodlum son, and a mysterious 15-year-old girl, who holds the key to the entire puzzle.

"The Case of the Christmas Counterfeiters is **Mike Mains's masterpiece**—easily the best NHDC novel so far."

"My 12yo son loved all three books in this series."

"My 10 year old son has enjoyed all three books. He just finished The Case of the Christmas Counterfeiters and loved it. He says 'It is intriguing and leaves you in suspense. When it seems that there is no hope, something cool happens! **I highly recommend this book!**' "

The Case of the Deadly Double-Cross

All Jeffrey wanted to do was help a friend from school find her missing father. He had no way of knowing it would lead to his being arrested for the man's murder. Now after a daring escape, he and his best friend Pablo must solve an impossible crime and catch a killer—before the police catch them.

"My 11 yr. old granddaughter loved this book (and the rest of the books in the series). **She raved about it so much that her college grad sister decided to read it also."**

"My 12 year old son read this book in 3 nights and ended up staying up very late because he couldn't put it down."

The Case of the Jilted Juliet

A mysterious note found in a school library book leads Jeffrey and his friends to suspect that a girl who committed suicide thirty years ago was actually murdered. Their investigation leads them to a quiet sixteen-year-old girl with a secret past, an ex-con with a motive for murder, and a list of suspects that includes their own high school principal.

"**Fabulous!** Teens and adults alike will love this **action-packed mystery.**"

"**Mike Mains has really outdone himself in his latest outing of the North Hollywood Detective Club.** Just when you think you've got it all figured out, fresh clues send mystery down a whole new path. Mains brings his characters to three-dimensional life and draws the entire neighborhood in rich detail."

The Great Adventure Book for Boys

Classic adventure tales for boys of all ages: *The Most Dangerous Game*, *Leiningen Versus the Ants*, and *The Hound of the Baskervilles*.

Monkey Jokes—A Joke Book for Kids!

Tickle your funny bone with these laugh-a-minute jokes for kids. Apes, cheetahs, gorillas, they're all here, ready to entertain you in the world's first and funniest collection of monkey jokes.

Are you ready for a gorillian laughs? Then stop monkeying around and get this book today!

World's Funniest Jokes for Kids!

Here they are, the world's funniest jokes and limericks all assembled in one book! Every joke and limerick in this book is personally kid-tested by yours truly! Buy this book today and start laughing tomorrow!

Annihilate Your Acne

Do you suffer from acne? Contrary to popular opinion, acne is caused by food allergies and environmental toxins. Eliminate those causes and acne melts away like a snow cone on a hot summer day.

www.ingramcontent.com/pod-product-compliance
Lightning Source LLC
Chambersburg PA
CBHW051755040426
42446CB00007B/369